The Cato Institute

The Cato Institute is named for the libertarian pamphlets *Cato's Letters*, which were inspired by the Roman Stoic Cato the Younger. Written by John Trenchard and Thomas Gordon, *Cato's Letters* were widely read in the American colonies in the early eighteenth century and played a major role in laying the philosophical foundation for the revolution that followed.

The erosion of civil and economic liberties in the modern world has occurred in concert with a widening array of social problems. These disturbing developments have resulted from a major failure to examine social problems in terms of the fundamental principles of human dignity, economic welfare, and justice.

The Cato Institute aims to broaden public policy debate by sponsoring programs designed to assist both the scholar and the concerned layperson in analyzing questions of political economy.

The programs of the Cato Institute include the sponsorship and publication of basic research in social philosophy and public policy; publication of major journals on the scholarship of liberty and commentary on political affairs; production of debate forums for radio; and organization of an extensive program of symposia, seminars, and conferences.

The Myth of
Social Cost

The Myth of Social Cost

Steven N. S. Cheung

With a Foreword by Ronald Hamowy

CATO PAPER No. 16

CATO
INSTITUTE
San Francisco, California

Library of Congress Cataloging in Publication Data

Cheung, Steven N   S
   The myth of social cost.

   (Cato paper ; no. 16)
   Originally published in 1978 by the Institute of Economic
Affairs, London.
    1. Externalities (Economics)   2. Welfare economics.
I. Title.   II. Series.
HB846.3.C47   1980   330.15′5   80-26083
ISBN 0-932790-21-6

Printed in the United States of America.

CATO INSTITUTE
747 Front Street
San Francisco, California 94111

CONTENTS

FOREWORD

The escalation of political intervention into economic life, which has reached massive proportions in the last half-century, probably owes more to the theory of social cost than to any other economic theory of government. Social-cost theory sets forth the thesis that voluntary exchanges between individuals often have as their byproduct costs to third parties not directly involved in these exchanges. These externalities, it is argued, often result in the spoliation of the land, the pollution of our air and water, the overexploitation of natural resources, and the overproduction of goods and services, all of which impose severe costs on large numbers of people who remain uncompensated by these private agreements. The suggested solution to this problem is government intervention in the economy to restrain the uninhibited operation of the marketplace and thereby directly impose these external costs on the parties who take part in any exchange. Regardless of what form government intrusion takes, from taxing certain activities to subsidizing others to completely suppressing still others, its ostensible aim is to discourage socially costly activities and to encourage socially beneficial ones, thus maximizing the socially efficient allocation of resources.

The Cambridge economist A. C. Pigou first systematically developed the theory of social cost in his *Economics of Welfare* (1920). In this work, Pigou offered an extensive analysis of possible inefficient situations, wherein private costs—costs borne solely by those privy to an exchange—and social costs diverged, thus requiring corrective government intervention. Pigou's analysis has since exerted tremendous influence on economists and has, in one form or another, become canonical. Its far-reaching implications have given proponents of wholesale government intervention in the economy an extremely potent rationale. It is, after all, possible to claim that every act has external effects and that, if the function of the state is to correct for these externalities, then the government may legitimately intrude into any aspect of social life.

In *The Myth of Social Cost*, Professor Steven Cheung of the University of Washington takes issue with this line of argument and with standard social-cost analysis, both on theoretical and empirical grounds. After treating the history of social-cost theory from Pigou through its more recent formulations, Professor Cheung rightly points out that many of the supposed problems posed by externalities are themselves the result of poorly defined or narrowly construed notions of property rights. If society's legal institutions more clearly delineated and policed property rights, many of the current external effects of economic transactions would become internalized and subject to contractual transfer.

Professor Cheung's most extensive criticism centers on the lack of any empirical evidence to support the conclusions arrived at by social-cost analysis. "Using imaginary 'facts' to support imaginary policies seems habitual in the Pigovian tradition," he writes. Yet, "not a single popular example has been supported by hard evidence." Indeed, the author argues that, when carefully examined, the two most commonly accepted examples alleged to indicate divergences between private and social costs strongly suggest that no such divergence in fact exists. In analyzing the relation between owner versus tenant cultivation and agricultural productivity and the relation between apple farming and beekeeping, Professor Cheung shows that traditional market arrangements have internalized the very externalities that social-cost theory insists are present. He concludes:

> In land tenure and in the activity of bees the alleged deficiencies of market arrangements are not supported by the evidence. Henry Sidgwick's classic example of the lighthouse as a public good from which users who will not pay cannot be excluded has recently been opened to question. Similarly, I contend that problems of environmental degradation diverge in essential aspects from what economists seem to believe. Even a close look into various forms of real-property transactions confirms that such factors as barking dogs and crying babies are duly considered in rental contracts for apartments, and that cleanliness and quietness are routinely valued in pricing.

This is, of course, not to deny that there are indeed numerous instances of uncontracted effects generated by private exchanges; it would clearly be counterintuitive to argue that externalities are not pervasive throughout society. But, as Professor Cheung observes, the presence of these effects is no indication of misallocation of resources and does not, in most cases, offer any justification for corrective government action.

Both economists and laymen are indebted to Professor Cheung for pointing out some of the problems associated with social-cost theory. The reader might well have wished for a more thorough theoretical examination of the whole notion of social cost—whether, in fact, the concept itself can stand up under rigorous scrutiny. The social cost of a transaction is putatively a measure of the total of individual costs borne by all those in any way affected by that transaction and, as such, rests on the questionable notions that the subjective utilities and disutilities of each individual are additive and that it is possible to determine a "cost" in the absence of a market. But these are problems that the author has chosen not to address. Even so, he has provided a useful critique of a dubious economic theory that has served as an excuse for governments to intervene when and where they will under the pretense of rationalizing the chaos of the marketplace.

September 1980   Ronald Hamowy
                                                  Edmonton, Alberta

PREFACE
to the 1978 Edition

The *Hobart Papers* are intended to contribute a stream of authoritative, independent, and lucid analysis to the understanding and application of economics to private and government activity. Their characteristic theme has been the optimum use of scarce resources and the extent to which it can best be achieved in markets within an appropriate framework of laws and institutions or, where markets cannot work or have disproportionate defects, by better methods with relative advantages or less decisive defects. Since the alternative to the market is, in practice, the state, and both are imperfect, the choice between them is effectively made on the judgment of the comparative consequences of "market failure" and "government failure."

The most damaging criticism of the market for some decades but especially in recent years has been that buyers and sellers who exchange goods and services by contract often create costs and benefits ("externalities") for third parties not directly involved in the exchange, so that the market suffers from a serious "failure" in these bargains. It generates excessive production of goods/services that impose costs on others who cannot be compensated, and insufficient of those that yield benefits to others for which they cannot be made to pay. From this diagnosis has followed a series of conclusions for policy varying from a structure of taxes (to discourage output with social/ external costs) and subsidies (to stimulate output with social/ external benefits) to suppression of the market entirely and its replacement by government.

For some years economists, especially in the United States, have contested the original diagnosis of externalities. They have offered alternative explanations of the supposed divergences between private and social costs/benefits. They have argued that the parties to private contracts will *not* fail to take the externalities into account in their dealing provided there are no barriers to "trading" in external effects. The newer conclusion for policy is the possibility of redrawing the boundaries of property rights so that such "trades" over external effects can take place. This new perspective on externalities has been slow to filter through to thinking on policy in the United Kingdom.

This paper presents this countercritique by American, and more recently British, economists on two planes. The central portion is the work of Professor Steven N. S. Cheung of the University of Washington, who has developed the countercritique in a series of studies known best in the United States. His argument is addressed chiefly to economic specialists in the subject who will find it a microcosm of his writings for some years brought up-to-date in the light of the latest developments in the debate between economists. He has explained his analysis by arithmetical tables designed to show alternative methods of measuring private and social costs. He follows the evolution of the theory of social cost/benefit from its originator of fifty years ago, the Cambridge economist A. C. Pigou, into its most recent forms, and claims that they are all defective. His essay is mainly intended for students and teachers of economics with special interest in the theory of social cost and externalities. His main conclusion is that the originators of "externality" theory relied on invalid assumptions and did not test their results. He holds that the evidence, when examined, reveals flaws in their reasoning. He joins issue both with Professor Pigou, on the basis of counter-evidence derived from land-tenure contracts and farming behavior in China, and with Professor J. E. Meade by contesting his analysis of the pollination and nectar extraction services of bees.

In view of the difficulty that newcomers to economics may have in following this closely reasoned analysis, we invited Professor Charles K. Rowley of the University of Newcastle upon Tyne, a British authority on this development in economics, to outline briefly the importance of Professor Cheung's analysis. Professor Rowley is, with Professor A. T. Peacock, the author of the deepest British economic study of the subject, *Welfare Economics: A Liberal Restatement*.[1] The opening sentence of

[1]London: Martin Robertson, 1975.

his Prologue graphically states his verdict: "Society might be far better off if the 'problem' of social cost had never been discovered." The importance of the economics of social cost is that it has considerably influenced British economists and other academics and the governments they have advised. Professor Rowley's exposition will be found easy to follow by beginners in economics and by noneconomists.

For readers interested in discussion of public policy, such as of various forms of environmental controls, we also invited Mr. John Burton to write a longer epilogue designed to apply Professor Cheung's central analysis more fully in language again suitable for the nonspecialist and to illustrate it by topical examples from Britain and overseas. Like Professor Rowley he indicates the alternative approach from the study of property rights and of public choice[2] as a more fundamental insight to the reasons for external effects and the naiveté of the proposals for policy drawn from the Pigovian analysis. Both British authors indicate the conclusions that follow for government policy from this superior perspective of property rights and public choice.

If our three authors are right, the continued teaching in Britain of the simplistic conventional approach to social cost/benefit is seriously flawed and dangerously misleading. A wide range of British policies from technological and industrial policies and the third London airport to town and country planning, subsidies for the arts, and measures for the protection of the environment are based on this flawed analysis. There is urgent need of reexamination in the light of the more realistic analysis presented in this paper.

The Institute's trustees, directors, and advisers do not necessarily share the analysis of the authors, but it is offered as a scholarly and severely realistic contribution, for both specialists and noneconomists, to the debate among economists and the advice they can properly give to policy makers.

August 1978   Arthur Seldon

---

[2] J. M. Buchanan and others, *The Economics of Politics* (London: Institute of Economic Affairs, Reading No. 18, 1978).

PROLOGUE
The "Problem" of Social Cost

CHARLES K. ROWLEY

*Professor of Economics,
University of Newcastle upon Tyne*

Society might be far better off if the "problem" of social cost had never been discovered.

Professor Cheung examines the "problem" of social cost explicitly within the framework of Paretian welfare economics (named after the Italian economist Vilfredo Pareto), which is based on the notion that each individual is the best judge of his own welfare but which says nothing about comparisons of welfare between individuals. Difficulties may arise when the economic activity of one individual or firm in consumption or production generates an effect ("externality"), beneficial or detrimental, on some other individual or firm that is not party to it. The private costs of the activity, which together with the associated private benefits determine the scale on which it operates, will then diverge from the "social" costs, which include the costs to others; and similarly with benefits. In consequence, the scale of the activity may be too large or too small to attain the social optimum.

Pigou's externality tax: the example of chimney smoke

The common example of such a divergence between private and social cost is that of factory smoke which harms people in the neighborhood. The issue is whether or not the rate of activity (and smoke discharge) is too high and, if so, by what mechanism it is best reduced. For forty years following the treatment by Pigou in *The Economics of Welfare* (1920)[1] and

---

[1] A. C. Pigou, *The Economics of Welfare* (1920; 4th ed., London: Macmillan & Co., 1932).

before the refutation by Professor R. H. Coase[2] in 1960, most economists accepted that it would be desirable

- to make the owner of the factory liable for the damage caused to people injured by the smoke, or
- to place a marginal tax on the factory owner varying with the amount of smoke he produced and equivalent in money terms to the marginal damage it would cause, or
- to exclude the factory from areas in which its smoke would harm others.

Since the Coase analysis economists have learned to be more cautious in analyzing social cost and drawing conclusions for policy from it.

First, social cost effects are mutual. Where A inflicts harm on B, the relevant question for policy is not simply: How should we *restrain* A? To avoid the harm to B would be to inflict harm on A. The relevant question is therefore: *Should A be allowed to harm B or B be allowed to harm A?* The task is to avoid the more serious harm.

Recognition of this mutual effect sets most economists at odds with the more extreme conservationists, who usually see only one of the two effects. And it explains, in part at least, why societies that are conscious of the environment nevertheless tolerate pollution. Suppose it were possible technically to improve the quality of the River Tees to a level which would support migratory fish. Clearly, this treatment would benefit frustrated fishermen who suffer from the ability of the households and industry of Teeside to use the river as an open sewer. But should the river be treated? Only, the economists would say, if the marginal cost of controlling the discharge of sewage proved to be less than the marginal benefit to the fishermen. "Friends of the Earth," in contrast, would not see such a comparison as relevant in determining policy. This major divergence of approach must lead to conflicting conclusions for policy.

Second, the existence of a problem of social cost in itself indicates the presence of "transaction" costs. Why else would individuals forgo the gains from exchange which always exist where there are externalities?

[2] R. H. Coase, "The Problem of Social Cost," *Journal of Law and Economics,* October 1960.

HOW TRANSACTION COSTS ARISE

Transaction costs may arise as a consequence of
- first, the inadequate specification of property rights;
- second, the nature of the externality;
- third, the number of bargainers; and/or
- fourth, the inadequacy of the institutions.

1. *Inadequate definition of property rights*

Many of the difficulties with social cost arise in resources which shift from being free to being scarce as a consequence of economic activity.[3] Clean air, for example, is slowly polluted as industry expands; river water is increasingly fouled by the domestic sewage of an expanding community. In such circumstances, the "property" rights to pollute or not to pollute may never have been determined, and owner and user (polluter) of the river or other properties may be unwilling to strike a bargain because neither will concede the right to the other. Without this initial delimitation of property rights, there will be no market transactions—exchange or "trade"—to transfer and recombine them. A clear-cut decision on property rights may thus itself be all that is required to resolve the difficulty.

2. *Uncertain effect of externality*

Where the externality itself is complex and even ambiguous, so that the individuals *do not know* whether an activity is detrimental or beneficial to themselves, it is impossible to strike a bargain.[4] Scientists may disagree about the long-term impact upon fish life and plankton of discharges of waste matter to the river. The inability of the individuals to strike a bargain is perhaps itself sufficient evidence that the externality is not relevant for policy. Further research may clarify the effects. Information costs invariably arise over externalities.

3. *Bargaining costs*

Transaction costs may frequently increase with the number of individuals, both as a result of increased difficulties in

[3]C. K. Rowley, "Pollution and Public Policy," in A. J. Culyer, ed., *Economic Policies and Social Goals* (London: Martin Robertson, 1974).

[4]P. Burrows, C. Rowley, and D. Owen, "The Economics of Accidental Oil Pollution by Tankers in Coastal Waters," *Journal of Public Economics* 3 (1974).

locating all involved and of accurately revealing their preferences. Holiday makers, for example, are both numerous and widely dispersed geographically, and they are conscious only periodically of the adverse welfare effects from fouled beaches. This complication may explain why it has taken so long for holiday makers and others to reduce the "degradation" or fouling of coastal waters by oil and sewage pollution, as in the *Torrey Canyon, Amoco Cadiz,* and *Eleni V* disasters.

On the assumption of zero transaction costs, Professor Coase argued that the efficient solution would be attained by bargaining irrespective of the initial delimitation of rights. Once there are transaction costs, the effects are less clear-cut. Dr. E. J. Mishan,[5] indeed, has argued that bargaining costs rise with the size of the group, so that the costs of achieving a solution are much higher if the large group initiates the bargaining than if the individual (in his example an offender) is forced to do so.

This argument is unconvincing.[6] Certainly bargaining costs may rise as the numbers affected increase, but this does not imply that the onus of placing the incentive to take the initiative itself necessarily affects the size of those costs. It is impossible to generalize at all about which settlement of rights will lead to the lower bargaining costs. There is little evidence, for example, to suggest that people who would like to use rivers for recreation have made active use of their riparian property rights to prevent the discharge of effluent into rivers.

4. *Failure of legal and political institutions*

Finally, the transaction costs of resolving an externality problem may be as high as a consequence of inadequate institutions. Inevitably, this issue has dominated the debate on policy.

What are the main issues on which controversy has centered?

There are two kinds of externality: the anticipated and persistent, and the accidental and periodic. The externality literature is dominated by the former, the anticipated and persistent; but it is the accidental and periodic that are of increasing

[5]E. J. Mishan, "Pareto Optimality and the Law," *Oxford Economic Papers,* November 1967.

[6]P. Burrows, "On External Costs and the Visible Arm of the Law," *Oxford Economic Papers,* March 1970.

relevance. The implications for policy are by no means the same. Compulsory insurance is an obvious additional instrument for dealing with accidental and periodic externalities. But what can be done about anticipated and persistent externalities?

INSTRUMENTS OF GOVERNMENT INTERVENTION

The most obvious instrument of policy, once property rights are established and bargaining has failed, is court action. In an ideal world, it would suffice. But, in practice, British courts are less than helpful. The decisions of the courts reflect a preoccupation with imposing damages for past events and a prejudice in favor of injunction for potentially continuing activities. Clearly, these interventions do not appear to be adequate. In such circumstances, government intervention will appear appropriate, and indeed the vast majority of the literature on externality has argued for its use. The instruments recommended range from a Pigovian tax through a Coase-type tax subsidy, to "public" (i.e., government) ownership of the offending activity (e.g., nuclear power stations). Whatever method of intervention is adopted, Professor Cheung's paper will warn the wary reader not to overlook four fundamental issues usually ignored in the writings of "welfare" economists who have not been reared in the modern traditions of public choice, Virginia blend.

Fundamental issues

First, no one should expect that governments will behave simply as social agencies whose sole or primary purpose is to maximize welfare. Research during the past decade (by Buchanan, Tullock, Breton, et alia) has confirmed lay suspicions that politicians maximize their own objectives, including power, income, ideology, and patronage subject to the "constraints" imposed by elections.[7] For the most part, politicians are interested in externalities for their own sake as much as alcoholics are interested in the profitability of brewers. In practice, the consumer interest in the environment is likely to be dominated

[7]This subject is discussed fully by economists and others in Buchanan, *The Economics of Politics.*

politically by producer interests, so that activities producing externalities adverse to consumers will be excessive.

Second, the evidence is mounting[8] that government sector interventions are themselves excessively costly. The bureaucracy necessarily involved in imposing the political will upon the populace always has an "opportunity cost" in activities forgone that could have benefited the public. But recent developments in the economics of bureaucracy[9] suggest that these costs have a natural stimulus to rise once the bureaucrats assert their independent influence. The costs of intervention will often exceed the benefits.

Third, government should not be assumed to command more knowledge than the individuals affected. The latter, at least in the absence of the free-rider problem, have every *incentive* to inform themselves. Government—politicians and bureaucrats—will do so only if votes are at stake. In general, government may prove to be willing to intervene, once accorded the power, in response to decisive voter groupings and dominant pressure groups and irrespective of the underlying efficiency criterion of the public interest.

Fourth, the implications for individual freedom should not be ignored when assessing the argument for government intervention. Freedom implies the right of any individual not to be coerced by any other individual. The supposed existence of "social cost" has been one of the foremost pretexts for which such freedom has been transgressed and by which the authority of government has been extended.

---

[8] As recent issues of *Public Choice* and *The Journal of Law and Economic* clearly indicate: published respectively by the Center for Study of Public Choice, Virginia Polytechnic Institute and State University, Blacksburg, Virginia, and the University of Chicago Law School.

[9] William A. Niskanen, *Bureaucracy and Representative Government* (New York: Aldine-Atherton, 1971), and *Bureaucracy: Servant or Master?* (London: IEA, Hobart Paperback 5, 1973); Gordon Tullock, *The Vote Motive* (London: IEA, Hobart Paperback 9, 1976); and *The Economics of Politics.*

The Myth of Social Cost

This paper is part of a larger body of research on contracts, financially supported by the National Science Foundation of the United States.

"...theories [should] be examined for their implications for observable behaviour, and these specific implications compared with observable behaviour....Not only were such specific implications not sought and tested, but there was a tendency, when there appeared to be the threat of an empirical test, to reformulate the theory to make the test ineffective....[Economists] did not anxiously seek the challenge of the facts..."

GEORGE J. STIGLER

("The Development of Utility Theory," *Journal of Political Economy,* October 1950)

1. Introduction

Any public policy designed to intervene in the operation of the market is usually defended on one of three grounds. First, activities such as prostitution or gambling may be suppressed on the ground that they are unethical. Second, a policy may be adopted to improve the distribution of income. Finally, activities may be regulated on the ground that they entail inefficient allocation of resources.

On ethics, economic theory must remain silent: No testable propositions can be put forward unless each individual's judgment is accepted as given. In the seemingly persuasive argument for redistribution of income, economic analysis has failed to produce a convincing measure of a net improvement in "welfare" when £1 of every £100 is taken from one person and given to another. Only on the argument for government actions to correct inefficient activities does economic analysis have much to say, and it provokes major controversies.

To accept or to deny the desirability of a public policy necessarily involves "normative" value judgments on whether it *should* (or should not) be adopted. Economic efficiency, on the other hand, can be defined in "positive" terms concerned with whether a certain activity *is* (or is not) efficient. The transition from positive analysis to normative argument on policy requires only the inference that efficient allocation of resources is desirable to society. This inference is easy to draw and, to most economists, easy to accept.

Activities alleged to entail inefficient allocation of resources range widely through monopoly, environmental degradation, the provision of public goods,[1] and so on. Diverse reasons have

---

[1] [Goods or services whose consumption by an additional person does not reduce the amount available to others. Classic examples include a lighthouse, a television show, and national defense.—ED.]

been offered for such market "failures," and economists differ on the appropriate remedies to be undertaken by the state. The disagreements usually stem not from conflicting analytical tools but rather from different assumptions. During the past eighteen years, research into the economics of property rights and the costs of making transactions has shown that the range of allegedly inefficient activities shares one common element: a divergence between private and social costs. Because this generalization permits a broader inquiry into the causes of the activities, it becomes possible, as well as important, to reexamine the arguments for or against using public policies as corrective devices.

Section 2 discusses the basic concepts of social cost as we understand them today. Section 3 evaluates four measures of the divergence between private and social costs and offers further examples to illustrate them. The reinterpretation of alleged market "failures" necessitates a discussion in section 5 of the essential conditions for economic explanation. Sections 4 and 6 comment on two common fallacies in the use of social-cost analysis to guide policy making. Section 7 concludes the paper.

2. The Basic Concepts in Social Cost

In 1897 Vilfredo Pareto enunciated a condition of resource allocation the significance of which was not fully appreciated in his time. There is, he said, a state of resource allocation in which:

> It [is] impossible to find a way of moving a very small distance from that position so that the ophelimite [gain or benefit] enjoyed by each individual increases....any small departure from that position necessarily causes an increase in ophelimite which some individuals enjoy and diminishes that which others enjoy: It will be agreeable to some and disagreeable to others.[2]

This statement defines what is now known as the Pareto condition: *a state where it is no longer possible to reallocate the use of resources so that one individual will gain without loss to another.* The term "economic efficiency" in its standard usage refers to the attainment of maximum aggregate value of goods and services, or maximum value of the scarce resources used to produce them. These values are taken as dictated by the preferences of the individuals involved. In a society, efficient resource allocation is equated with the Pareto condition, which thus offers a more illuminating way of evaluating one state of resource allocation with another than that of asking whether some maximum *value* is attained. Instead it asks whether some *individual* can be made to gain without loss to another.

---

[2]This quotation is taken from Everett Johnson Burtt, Jr., *Social Perspectives in the History of Economic Theory* (New York: St. Martin's Press, 1972), p. 274. In Burtt's translation, the ending of the first sentence reads "...each individual increases or decreases." This phrase makes no sense and may be the result of a misprint.

Robinson Crusoe always efficient

A central postulate in economic analysis is that each individual will maximize his real income (or gain) subject to limitations or "constraints," the term used here to include all the factors which restrain an individual from achieving an infinitely high income. They comprise four groups: (1) scarcity of resources; (2) diminishing returns—nature's law which dictates that one cannot produce an infinite quantity of grain by continuing to add fertilizer to a given piece of land; (3) property rights, which stem from competition for the same resources; and (4) transactions costs, which include the costs of searching, negotiating, and enforcing contracts, and of defining and policing of rights; (3) and (4) are found only in a *society*.

It is almost impossible to envisage inefficiency in a one-man (or "Robinson Crusoe") economy. Crusoe will maximize the value of goods and services he produces for himself, subject to the strictures of his scarce resources and the law of diminishing returns. If he errs in a decision, miscalculates the weather, or forgets what he has planned, he fails only because he is constrained by the lack of foresight, information, or know-how, which are scarce resources in themselves. In other words, Crusoe is *always* efficient, if we adequately assess the constraints.

If inefficiency is difficult to envisage in a Crusoe economy, why is it so easy to perceive in a society? If each individual is thought of as a "constrained maximizer," that is, he tries to achieve the best possible result from his efforts, how is it possible to produce situations where the Pareto condition is violated? The answer, we will show later, concerns largely the optical state of economists whose imagination is myopic in one direction and too far-sighted in another.

In the schema (or "paradigm") of neoclassical economics: Given a set of assumed constraints, efficient allocation of resources is attained when the additional ("marginal") net gain to society is zero and where the total real income generated by the scarce resources is at a maximum. Depending on the inherent variables, the sets of marginal equalities necessary to produce an efficient solution may vary from one analysis to another. In a society these equal-marginal sets may become so immensely complicated that it is natural to conceive of situations where certain marginal values are not equated with one another. The economist chiefly responsible for envisaging such inefficient situations and popularizing them was Professor A. C. Pigou of Cambridge.

Pigou's private and social costs

In two successive classic works on welfare,[3] Pigou analyzed various inefficient situations in terms of what has become known as divergence between private and social costs. Like the Pareto condition, the "divergence" applies only to society as a whole, but it provides a frame of reasoning within which an economist may stretch his imagination far and wide in evaluating the state of the economy. Above all, it yields apparently easy prescriptions for corrective government actions. After one lesson on Pigou, a newcomer may feel he knows how to improve the world.

The popularity and acceptance of Pigou's thesis is rather remarkable since much of his original analysis makes difficult and confusing reading. Nonetheless a fairly clear version of what Pigou seemed to say is illustrated in his classic example of a polluting factory (to which Pigou gave exactly one sentence of passing reference).[4] We shall use numerical values to examine all the basic principles.

Suppose the owner of a shoe factory can increase the output of products by increasing the input of resources. For simplicity (only), let us suppose that one type of input, say labor, is increased while other cooperating types (capital, etc.) are held constant. The input units are shown in table A, column 1. Column 2 represents the incremental or marginal value of the shoe output, with the word "private" denoting a return that can be captured by the factory owner through contracted transactions with shoe consumers. This value is calculated by multiplying a constant market price per pair of shoes by the physical outputs produced by each incremental unit of input; the law of diminishing returns dictates that the value falls as input increases. The cumulative sum (not shown) of the *marginal* values in column 2 represents the value of *total* private product at each

[3] *Wealth and Welfare* (1912); and *The Economics of Welfare*.
[4] *The Economics of Welfare*, p. 160–61.

TABLE A

(1)	(2)	(3)	(4)	(5)	(6)	(7)	(8)	(9)
Input	Value of Marginal Private Product	Marginal Private Input Cost	Marginal Private Gain	Total Economic Waste	Value of Marginal Uncontracted Effects	Marginal Social Cost	Marginal Social Gain	Total Social Economic Waste
	£	£	£	£	£	£	£	£
0	0	0	0	56	0	0	0	24
1	26	12	14	42	– 2	14	12	12
2	24	12	12	30	– 4	16	8	4
3	22	12	10	20	– 6	18	4	0
4	20	12	8	12	– 8	20	0	0
5	18	12	6	6	– 10	22	– 4	4
6	16	12	4	2	– 12	24	– 8	12
7	14	12	2	0	– 14	26	– 12	24
8	12	12	0	0	– 16	28	– 16	40
9	10	12	– 2	2	– 18	30	– 20	60
10	8	12	– 4	6	– 20	32	– 24	84
11	6	12	– 6	12	– 22	34	– 28	112

amount of input. That is, if three units of input are employed, the total private product is £72, the sum of £26 + £24 + £22.

The marginal private cost in column 3 represents the cost to the factory owner of employing additional (marginal) units of input. For simplicity, it is assumed to be constant throughout at £12 (in our case, the wage rate for labor). The cumulative sum (again not shown) of the marginal values here represents the total labor cost. The marginal private product *net* of marginal private cost, or the difference between columns 2 and 3, is the marginal private gain (column 4). This gain is not a profit but a payment to all *other* inputs including the factory owner's self-employed efforts. The *total* gain reaches a maximum of £56 at eight units of input, where the value of private marginal product equals the marginal private cost (£12 = £12). The postulated motive of maximization (subject to constraints) dictates that the factory owner will operate at this quantity of output. The explicit constraints here include the cost of inputs, the diminishing returns, and the state of technology. Other relevant constraints are only implicit: that the prices of input and output are determined costlessly in the markets; that the producer has no difficulty in finding and negotiating with his customers; that the workers, once contracted, will work exactly as agreed; and the list may go on to include the weather, health, and the like.

The values of economic "waste" are listed in column 5. These values represent the *losses* in *total* gains at different amounts of production.[5] Thus, if input is zero and therefore output is also zero, the maximum total gain of £56 which could be obtained by employing eight units of inputs will now be lost and hence wasted; at three units of inputs, the total gain of £36 is less than the maximum gain of £56 by a waste of £20. What is a gain from one view is a waste from another view: These are two sides of the same coin. Thus constrained maximization by the factory owner produces a situation where economic waste is zero. The efficiency of using eight units of input may be interpreted in another way. Column 2 represents the *maximum* values the customers are willing to pay for the marginal shoe

[5]There are other measures of economic waste if the analysis is broadened to include other sectors of the economy, but this expansion is not yet important in this paper.

outputs generated by the use of marginal inputs; column 3 represents the *maximum* values of alternative production for-gone in employing the marginal inputs for shoe production. When these two values are equated at the margin, it becomes impossible to reallocate any input resource in shoe production so as to benefit both the customer and the factory owner. The Pareto condition is thus satisfied.

Pigou's central thesis: the polluting factory

We now introduce the central thesis of Pigou's argument. Suppose that the factory emits smoke which pollutes the environment, thereby inflicting damage on the neighborhood which is not subject to contracting; thus no transaction takes place between the factory owner and the residents. The value of these *uncontracted* effects per increment of input is listed in table A, column 6, where negative signs indicate that the effects are damaging. We add the absolute values of columns 3 and 6 to obtain the marginal *social* cost in column 7. That is, the marginal damage inflicted on the neighbors (column 6) is here viewed as part of the marginal resource cost to society in the production of shoes; it is combined with the marginal cost incurred by the factory owner in hiring marginal inputs (column 3) to form the marginal social cost. On the other hand, we subtract the value in column 7 from that in column 2 to obtain the marginal *social* gain in column 8.

One interpretation of a divergence between private and social costs is the difference between columns 7 and 3. (This difference equals column 6 with signs omitted.) Pigou himself never used the phrase "divergence between private and social costs"; he referred to "divergences between marginal social net product and marginal [private] net product."[6] By this he was probably referring to the difference between columns 8 and 4, which turns out to be exactly the same as our earlier measure of the divergence between private and social costs (column 6 with signs omitted). In other words, *the uncontracted effects alone account for the divergence.*

The *total* social gain reaches a maximum of £24 at four units

---

[6]This is the title of his classic chapter *(Economics of Welfare* (1920), chap. 6; 3rd ed., part 2, chap. 9).

of inputs, where the *marginal* social gain is zero (column 8). However, if the factory owner operates at eight units of inputs so as to obtain the maximum *private* gain, the total *social* gain will be a negative of £16 (a cumulative sum, which here by coincidence equals the marginal social gain). This total social gain need not, of course, have a negative value; but under private maximization, and given the harmful uncontracted effects, it will necessarily be less than the maximum of £24 at four units of input. Here, then, is Pigou's central argument. The shoe factory owner, if left to pursue his own gain, will not take into account the effects of the pollution. Hence "over-production" will result. To attain efficiency, the factory owner's behavior must therefore be altered by such "corrective" government actions as taxation, compulsory compensation to the neighbors, regulation of the amount either of shoe production or of pollution, or entire elimination of the factory.

In column 9 we calculate the total value of social economic waste (i.e., with uncontracted effects included) in the same way that economic waste was derived in column 5. When the factory operates at eight units of inputs the social economic waste is £40 and it can be demonstrated that the Pareto condition is violated. If instead of eight units of inputs only four units are employed, the factory owner loses £12 (£6 + £4 + £2 in column 4), but the damage inflicted on the neighborhood is reduced by £52 (£10 + £12 + £14 + £16 in column 6). The difference between £52 and £12 is a net gain of £40. Hence all parties, including the factory owner, may gain from the reallocation of resources.

This argument may appear persuasive but it fails to press the question: Under private maximization, and in the absence of corrective policies, what constraints may lead to, or away from, the decision to use four units of input? To specify such constraints (particularly in a way useful for testing hypotheses) turns out to be very difficult. Yet failure to answer this question means that when we say the manufacturer will determine to use eight units of input we are merely *asserting* a result rather than deriving it from examination of costs and gains at varying amounts of inputs. (We return to this topic in section 4.)

TABLE B
A TALE OF FOUR ECONOMISTS

(1)	Pigou's Balance		Unit Price of Output	Viner's Balance		Coase's Balance		Cheung's Balance	
	(2)	(7)	(10)	(11)	(12)	(4)	(6)	(3)	(13)
Input	Value of Marginal Private Product	Marginal Social Cost	Unit Price of Output	Marginal Private Output Cost	Marginal Social Output Cost	Marginal Private Gain	Value of Marginal Uncontracted Effects	Marginal Private Input Cost	Marginal Social Effects
	£	£	£	£	£	£	£	£	£
0	0	0	1.00	0	0	0	0	0	0
1	26	14	1.00	0.46	0.54	14	− 2	12	24
2	24	16	1.00	0.50	0.67	12	− 4	12	20
3	22	18	1.00	0.55	0.82	10	− 6	12	16
4	20	20	1.00	0.60	1.00	8	− 8	12	12
5	18	22	1.00	0.67	1.22	6	−10	12	8
6	16	24	1.00	0.75	1.50	4	−12	12	4
7	14	26	1.00	0.86	1.86	2	−14	12	0
8	12	28	1.00	1.00	2.33	0	−16	12	− 4
9	10	30	1.00	1.20	3.00	− 2	−18	12	− 8
10	8	32	1.00	1.50	4.00	− 4	−20	12	−12
11	6	34	1.00	2.00	5.67	− 6	−22	12	−16

3. A Tale of Four Economists

In at least four different ways, gains and costs can be balanced *at the margin* to yield a maximum social gain of £24 from the use of four units of input. In effect, the four ways of approaching the question are equivalent; they merely represent different angles of examining the problem. But since confusion over these viewpoints has led to wide disagreement among economists seeking to develop theories of "social cost," students of the subject will be interested in examining the four approaches.

The four methods, used by four economists including me, are illustrated in table B, where column 1 again indicates the level of input.

1. *Pigou's Input Tax*

The first method, employed by Pigou,[7] involves the use of columns 2 and 7 from table A. Column 2 represents the marginal return of shoe production that can be captured by the factory owner; column 7 is the marginal cost to society, including both the marginal input cost and the marginal damage inflicted. These two values are equated (£20 = £20) at four units of input. If in maximizing private gain the factory owner operates at eight units of input, Pigou's balance shows that the social cost exceeds the private return by £16 at the margin. Efficiency will therefore be improved by *restraining* the owner's behavior to reduce his input by such devices as taxation or compulsory compensation to the neighbors.

Pigou himself, however, was ambiguous on the specific form

---

[7]It is not clear whether Pigou was using this or any other method, although this seems to fit best with his discussion. Pigou was mainly concerned with *divergence* at the margin, not with *balance* at the margin. Furthermore, in his numerous examples marginal consideration is seldom evident. (*Economics of Welfare,* chaps. 6, 7, and 8.)

and magnitude of taxation or compensation.[8] Pigou's balance seems to indicate that the most obvious form of taxation or compulsory compensation would be an imposition of £8 on each unit of *input* (the difference between £20 and £12 in column 2). When each value in column 2 is reduced by £8, the factory owner's marginal return at four units of input will be £12, which equals the marginal private input cost (table A, column 3). The owner's input is thus reduced to the four units consistent with maximum social gain.

2. *Viner's Output Tax*

A more popular method of balancing marginal gains and costs was probably made familiar in a classic paper by Jacob Viner.[9] It is illustrated in (new) columns 10, 11, and 12 in table B. Here, input values are translated into output (product) values. For simplicity, we assume a constant price of £1.00 for each pair of shoes (column 10). The marginal private *output* cost (column 11) is calculated by dividing column 3 by column 2 (see table A). Private gain is, as with Pigou, maximized at eight units of input where the price of output, or the marginal receipt to the shoe producer, equals the marginal private output cost. On the other hand, the marginal *social* output cost, which includes the pollution damage, is in column 12, a value calculated by dividing column 7 by column 2 (see table A). The maximization of social gain now requires the marginal balancing of output price and social output cost, where at four units of input we have £1.00 = £1.00.

The ready acceptance by economists of this second balancing method may be attributed to the neatness of its taxing policy: A simple tax of 40p on the sale of each pair of shoes will raise each value in column 11 by 40p, thus making a triple marginal equality at four units of inputs, £1.00 = £1.00 = £1.00. The economic waste in the absence of any such corrective device is also easy to see. If eight units of input are employed under unregulated private maximization, the marginal social output cost of shoes exceeds its price by £1.33 (£2.33 − £1.00). Since

[8]Ibid., p. 168 and ff.

[9]"Cost Curves and Supply Curves," *Zeitschrift für Nationalökonomie* (1931), pp. 23–46, reprinted in George J. Stigler and Kenneth Boulding, eds., *Readings in Price Theory* (Homewood, Ill.: Richard D. Irwin, 1952).

the price is the maximum value customers are willing to pay for the "last" pair of shoes produced, £1.33 is the waste associated with the marginal pair. Restraint imposed by the 40p tax eliminates this waste. In other words, it removes the divergence between private and social costs, here measured by the difference between column 11 and column 12.

3. *Coase's Transaction*

Professor R. H. Coase advanced a third method of balancing. In his monumental 1960 paper,[10] he proposed a balance similar to the use of columns headed 4 and 6 in table B, reproduced from table A. Balancing the marginal gain to the factory owner against the negative marginal effect inflicted upon the neighborhood requires that the two marginal values be placed on the same side of the scale. At four units of inputs, where the social gain is at a maximum, we have £8 + (− 8) = £0. With this method it is hard to see any divergence between private and social costs; indeed, this difficulty seems to have misled Coase into ignoring the concept and arguing that his measure departs from tradition. However unfamiliar his method may be, it remains merely one of the four equivalents. His method of weighing the gain for one party against the loss of another does nevertheless provide a slight change of view which yields important and novel results. We shall elaborate on this in section 4.

Coase's method of balancing reveals yet another way of restraining the factory owner to limit his input to four units. To compensate his neighbors fully (but barely) for the damage, the factory owner will pay them the marginal value (omitting signs) of column 6 for each successive unit of input. He will be willing to pay up to the fourth unit of input and no more, since if he were to employ a fifth unit his gain (£6) would be less than the requisite compensation (£10). If exacted by the government, this system of payment would become a structure of taxation that would also limit input to four units.

It is interesting to note that the form of taxation or compensation associated with the Pigou, Viner, and Coase balancing methods requires different *total* payments from the factory owner. First, the Pigou tax of £8 per unit of input will place the total payment for using four units of input at £32. Second, the

---

[10]Coase, "The Problem of Social Cost," pp. 1–44.

Viner 40p unit tax on output pegs the total payment at £36.80, since four units of input yield a total output of ninety-two units. Third, the tax structure defined by column 6 will impose a total tax of £20 for the use of four units of input. What is the *same* in all three cases is the tax at the input *margin*. With the Pigou and Coase methods, the amount of tax for the use of the fourth unit of input is £8. With the Viner method, the output generated by the fourth unit of input is twenty, which when multiplied by the 40p tax per unit of output again yields £8 per unit of input.

Indeed, if compulsory compensation or taxation is to be extracted from the factory owner to restrain his use of input to four units, the *total* amount paid by him may vary in a wide range. The *minimum* total amount is zero, when the factory owner is subjected to a marginal input tax of £8 only if his use of input goes beyond the fourth unit. The *maximum* total amount is to compel the owner to give his entire factory away freely to the neighbors, who then—operating the factory to maximize their gains (and abstracting from other constraints not specified in our illustration)—will limit the use of input to four units. Conversely, if the neighbors are compelled to give their properties away freely to the factory owner, to maximize his total gain, including the gain in value of the neighboring properties, the owner will again limit the use of input to four units. As we shall see, this point, however obvious, is the crux of what is now known as the Coase theorem.

4. *Cheung's Aggregated Balance*

We now turn to a fourth balancing method which I proffer as an alternative. In table B this balance involves the use of column 3 from table A and a new column 13. The values in column 13 are calculated by adding the marginal private returns of using inputs (column 2) to the marginal uncontracted effects (column 6) to obtain the marginal social effects. Column 13 may therefore be viewed as presenting the values of marginal social product reached as input increases. At four units of input, where again social gain is at a maximum, private cost and social return are balanced at the marginal, £12 = £12. Given the information provided by columns 3 and 13, it is highly difficult to derive any corrective tax or compulsory-compensation scheme, which perhaps explains why this method has been neglected. But the deficiency is more than made up by the simplicity and generality of this fourth approach. Let me explain.

Every individual action generates a spectrum of effects, each of which may impose effects upon others. The fourth method of evaluating that action in economic terms is to balance the cost of the action incurred by the performer against the sum of the values of its generated effects, including those contracted and those not. Whether the effects command a positive value (such as the value of shoes) or a negative value (such as pollution), the Pareto condition is satisfied whenever the cost and the return balance at the margin. The presence of uncontracted effects such as pollution may result in an imbalance, but this is viewed simply as a situation where the marginal cost of an action deviates from its marginal returns, *without regard to any divergence between private and social costs.* In other words, however varied the effects of an action may be, their values may be similarly aggregated, and the return and cost of the action can then be balanced in a way similar to that where uncontracted effects are absent.

Let us turn to some examples other than the polluting factory. It is well known that the uncontracted effects of an action may be beneficial, as in the classic example of apple farming and beekeeping.[11] An apple orchard produces not only apples but also nectar, and a neighboring beekeeper is said to collect nectar from the apple blossoms free of charge. In maximizing his private gain, it is argued, the orchard owner will not take into account the valuable nectar his apple blossoms bestow upon the beekeeper. Hence apples will be "under-produced," and to attain maximum social gain a "corrective" subsidy must be granted to apple farming or a compulsory compensation paid by the beekeeper to the orchard owner. (We return to this example in a different context in section 6.)

Uncontracted effects and unjustified government action: the case of the piano player

Less publicized, but far more important, is another case where the uncontracted effects imposed by one party upon

[11] J. E. Meade, "External Economies and Diseconomies in a Competitive Situation," *Economic Journal,* March 1952, pp. 54–67.

another start out with positive value, decline to zero, and then become negative. My favorite example concerns Individual A, who plays the piano in his own home so that Neighbor B can hear him loud and clear. The length of time A plays per day is determined by equating the marginal value of piano playing to him with his marginal cost in time. Even though B is a music lover, there will be a point at which he finds A's excessive playing a nuisance.

We illustrate this case by retaining the values in columns 1 to 3 in table A, except that we now interpret the input units as hours of piano playing, and the value of marginal private product as the marginal value to the piano player of enjoying his own music. Columns 1 and 3 are shown in table C, with column 3 now representing the per-hour time-cost to the piano player. Column 6a is a variation of column 6, with the uncontracted marginal value of music to the neighbor turning into a nuisance beyond eight hours of play. We calculated the values in column 13a by aggregating the values in columns 2 (table A) and 6a for each amount of input. In table C, columns 3 and 13a form our fourth balance, and these marginal values are again equated at eight units of input, £12 = £12. The total social gain reaches a maximum of £140 (not shown) at eight units of input, or where the total social economic waste (column 9a) is zero. The values of the waste here (column 9a) may be obtained in the same manner as for column 9, or by summing the differences between columns 3 and 13a. Each difference represents a waste at the input margin.

It will be recalled that under private maximization the scale of operation will be at eight units of input. But in table C, the maximum social gain is attained also at eight units of input! This means that the piano player who *totally disregards* the effects of his music upon the neighbor happens to satisfy the Pareto condition (section 2, p. 5), and any tax or compulsory compensation will produce an *inefficient* result. The double maximum at eight units of input is, of course, strategically arranged to illustrate an important point. We place a zero value for the marginal uncontracted effects at eight units of input. This allows the demonstration that no matter how large the total value of uncontracted effects may be, the Pareto condition will be satisfied if at the private-maximizing margin the

TABLE C

(1)	(3)	(6a)	(13a)	(9a)
Input	Marginal Private Input Cost	Value of Marginal Uncontracted Effects	Marginal Social Effects	Total Social Economic Waste
	£	£	£	£
0	0	0	0	140
1	12	21	47	105
2	12	18	42	75
3	12	15	37	50
4	12	12	32	30
5	12	9	27	15
6	12	6	22	5
7	12	3	17	0
8	12	0	12	0
9	12	− 3	7	5
10	12	− 6	2	15
11	12	− 9	− 3	30

value of the *marginal* uncontracted effects is zero.[12] The presence of uncontracted effects, taken by itself, is thus no indication of misallocation of resources. And a divergence between private and social cost, unless referred specifically to the margin at which the action is carried, is therefore *no* justification for corrective government action.[13]

[12]Further elaboration is in James M. Buchanan and W. Craig Stubblebine, "Externality," *Economica,* November 1962, pp. 371–84; and Steven N. S. Cheung, "A Theory of Inter-individual Effects," Institute for Economic Research, University of Washington, 1972.

[13]Other important implications may be derived. If the values of marginal private product (column 2) and marginal uncontracted effects (column 6a) vary linearly with inputs, as in our illustration, it can be proved that the total value of social economic waste will necessarily fall when the value of the marginal uncontracted effects is positive and falling; conversely, the waste will rise if the value of these effects is negative and falling. Whether the values in columns 2 and 6a vary linearly with input or not, a definite implication is that the more closely the above marginal value approaches zero, the lower will be the total economic waste.

We may extend these implications to changes in the observable property values. In table C, at eight units of inputs the total benefit received by neighbor

Airports: commercial benefits as well as noise nuisances

Let us turn to a familiar situation of more general concern. It is evident that an airport introduces noise and pollution in its locality. Yet almost without exception the values of properties adjacent to an airport *rise* with its inception.[14] Presumably no one enjoys having dishes vibrating on the dinner table or babies screaming in the middle of the night. But the airport also produces such neighborhood *benefits* as an increase in business activities and a rising demand for lodging. To the extent that the beneficial effects outweigh the detrimental effects in value, the property values rise. If the aggregate value of all the uncontracted effects generated by the airport is positive, and if increasing air traffic leads to further increase in this value, any public policy adopted to curb the air traffic implies a movement away from the Pareto condition. Thus there is no defense on efficiency grounds for citing only the *harmful* uncontracted effects of airports and ignoring the *beneficial* ones. (In the United States this has been the dominant view popularized by the champion of consumers, Mr. Ralph Nader.)

The airport example is not, of course, unique. A school building in a residential area is comparable. Although the noise and disorder of the schoolchildren constitute a nuisance, the proximity of the school may be itself a benefit which will result in a rise in the values of neighboring properties. Indeed, one could ponder whether the classic polluting factory might not also generate more than enough beneficial uncontracted effects to justify, on efficiency grounds, a subsidy which would cause it to pollute (i.e., to produce) more!

B as a result of A's action is 84, the sum of the marginal values in column 6a. This benefit is an income which will be capitalized to the neighbor's property value. If the functions in columns 2 and 6a are linear, then when an increase in the observable input is accompanied by a rise in the observable property value, the total economic waste must be falling; and conversely when the affected property value is falling. Independent of linearity, a definite implication is that, other things equal, the lower the observable rate of change in property value effected by an observable change in input, the lower will be the total economic waste. (Further implications are discussed in Cheung, ibid.)

[14]Professor Alan Walters, who has conducted considerable research in the economics of airports, offered me this information.

Should monopoly be excluded from social cost analysis?

The divergence between private and social costs, reduced to its bare essence, refers to a situation where, *for some reason* (section 4), the cost and the benefit of an action fail to balance at some margin in a multi-individual world. Equivalent to a violation of the Pareto condition, it encompasses *all* allegedly inefficient situations in society.

Monopoly is usually treated as a source of economic waste separate from social cost. This separation is not always defensible. The output of the shoe factory carries two types of effects—the contractually transacted shoes and the uncontracted effects of the pollution—and inefficiency is said to arise from the latter. Suppose the factory is a monopolist. Ignoring pollution, inefficiency is then said to arise from the production of shoes alone in any case where the monopolist, in maximizing private gain, decides to produce to a point where the marginal benefit of shoes to consumers exceeds the associated marginal cost. However, there is a difference only in degree, not in concept, between the two cases where:

(i) market transactions or contractual arrangements are totally absent for some effects, as is allegedly the case for pollution; and

(ii) market transactions are available for a good but the contractual arrangements somehow fail to reach a condition where social gain is maximized.

Again, in the case of a "public" good, or a good amenable to concurrent use by many people without additional cost, such as a lighthouse or a television program, it has been accepted as a foregone conclusion that its production fails to equate the private cost and the social benefit at the margin. For some reason, efficient contracting is not attained.

For what reason? To say that a factory owner will not be concerned with his polluted neighborhood, a beekeeper will not pay for the orchard's nectar, or a television viewer will take a "free ride," is simply to say, self-evidently, that every individual wants to capture beneficial effects and to push away harmful ones. But to assert that he is able to do so *freely* is to claim that the world is without constraints. At what margin the performer of an action will operate can neither be determined nor explained without an appropriate specification of the constraints involved.

Furthermore, economists who propose corrective policies tend implicitly to assume unrealistic constraints on governments. It is assumed, for example, not only that situations exist which entail divergences between private and social costs, but also that some state agency will incur a sufficiently *low,* if not *zero,* cost in correctly assessing the values of various marginal schedules, even for complex situations where multiple uncontracted effects will have an impact on large numbers of individuals. The blithe assumption of low costs of government is further extended to the administration and enforcement of the proposed policy. And finally, in the event that a subsidy or a tax is proposed, it is assumed that the provision of tax funds or the appropriation of their proceeds will not, in themselves, lead to further problems of resource allocation and income distribution.

4. The Fallacy
in Specifying Constraints

The validity of assumptions in economic analysis has been a confusing issue. An "assumption" sometimes refers to a *postulate* which cannot be observed, and it is pointless then to question its reality.[15] Where constraints are observable, the term may refer to a simplification made necessary because no report of finite length can fully describe the observation. Relaxing such an assumption usually will not alter the essential result, and how drastic a simplification to make is often a matter of arbitrary judgment. Finally, the assumption may refer to a set of constraints, or a set of conditions, specified for the testing of a hypothesis, and "reality" means that the specified constraints conform in essential aspects with those in the real world. However simplified the constraints may be, this conformity to reality must be achieved if the implications are to be testable empirically. If a laboratory test calls for the use of a clean test tube, it will not do to "assume" that a dirty test tube is clean.

The unreality of social cost analysis: Pigou's two roads

Assuming constraints that fail to conform essentially to reality has been a major fallacy in the analysis of social cost, illustrated by Pigou's example of two roads:

> Suppose there are two roads ABD and ACD both leading from A to D. If left to itself, traffic would be so distributed that the trouble involved in driving a "representative" cart along each of the two roads would be equal.

[15]The well-known debate on the use of assumptions in economics in the 1950s and 1960s seems to have little to do with reality. The central issue of this debate is that, if A implies B, to say that "not A implies not B" commits the fallacy of denying the antecedent. Whether or not the antecedent A (called "assumption") is an observable entity was not a matter of prime concern.

> But, *in some circumstances,* it would be possible, by shift-
> ing a few carts from route B to route C, greatly to lessen
> the trouble of driving those still left on B, while only
> slightly increasing the trouble of driving along C. In these
> circumstances a rightly chosen measure of differential tax-
> ation against road B would create an "artificial" situation
> superior to the "natural" one. But the measure of dif-
> ferentiation must be rightly chosen.[16] (My italics.)

The phrase "in some circumstances" is similar to our earlier
phrase "for some reason," which in one stroke rules out the
necessity of specifying the constraints involved. Against this
soft spot Professor F. H. Knight launched his attack.[17]

Knight interpreted Road C as one which is "broad...
without crowding...but is poorly graded and surfaced," and
Road B as "a much better road but narrow and quite limited in
capacity."[18] If we interpret "the trouble involved in driving"
as simply the driving time of getting from Location A to Location D, and assume that the two roads are of equal length, no
one will use Road C in trying to reduce driving time unless congestion is developed to a degree on Road B. With traffic increasing on Road B and the drivers slowing one another down,
at some point the driving time in using either road will be the
same. Thus, any further congestion on Road B will shift traffic
toward the poorer Road C. Taxing the use of B and thereby
forcing some drivers to use C will result in no loss at all for
these drivers (since C is uncongested), but the remaining users
of Road B will stand to gain.

Professor Knight accepted this conclusion, but he wrote:

> The [conclusion] does in fact indicate what would happen
> if *no one owned the superior* [road]. But under private ap-
> propriation and self-seeking exploitation of the [roads]
> the course of events is very different. It is in fact the social
> function of ownership to prevent this excessive [use of the
> superior road]. Professor Pigou's logic in regard to the
> roads is, as logic, quite unexceptionable. Its weakness is
> one frequently met with in economic theorising, namely,

---

[16]Pigou, *Economics of Welfare,* p. 194.

[17]"Some Fallacies in the Interpretation of Social Costs," *Quarterly Journal of
Economics,* August 1924, pp. 582–606; reprinted in Stigler and Boulding, pp.
160–79. Hereafter we use the reprint for page references.

[18]Ibid., p. 162.

> that the assumptions diverge in essential respects from the facts of real economic situations.... If the roads are assumed to be subject to private appropriation and exploitation, precisely the ideal situation which would be established by the imaginary tax will be brought about through the operation of ordinary economic motives.[19]

Thus, among the "circumstances" which Pigou chose not to specify is the nature of *property rights* governing the use of the roads; but property rights are indispensable constraints for *any* decision involving more than one individual. Moreover, Knight was essentially correct in pointing out that if private ownership is established,

> the owner of the narrow road can charge for its use a toll representing its "superiority" over the free road, [and] in accordance with the theory of rent,...the toll will exactly equal the ideal tax...[20]

In charging the market with failure to attain the maximum social benefit while disallowing private property rights (upon which all private transactions must be based), Pigou was indeed barking up the wrong tree.

To my knowledge Pigou never replied to Knight's paper, although the example of the two roads was deleted from later editions of *The Economics of Welfare;* the debate was over when it had barely begun. This, together with the difficult nature of Knight's paper, may explain the slow progress of social-cost analysis in spite of numerous writings on the subject. It was not until the publication of Coase's paper thirty-six years later that the issue at stake was again brought into academic debate.

Coase's reciprocity and compensation (transaction) thesis

Turning to Coase's argument, we retain the example of the polluting factory, reproducing in table D Coase's method of balancing marginal values (columns 4 and 6). It will be recalled that at four units of input, where the marginal balance is £8 + (– £8) = £0, the total social gain is at a maximum. Balancing the gain to the factory owner (column 4) against the

[19]Ibid., pp. 163–64.
[20]Ibid., p. 164.

TABLE D

(1)	Coase's Balance		If B Has Right to Exclude Damage			If A Has Right to Inflict Damage		
	(4)	(6)	(14)	(15)	(16)	(17)	(18)	(19)
Input	Marginal Private Gain	Value of Marginal Uncontracted Effects	Maximum A willing to pay B	Minimum B willing to accept	Difference: Gain from Contracting	Maximum B willing to pay A	Minimum A willing to accept	Difference: Gain from Contracting
	£	£	£	£	£	£	£	£
0	0	0	44	20	24			
1	14	− 2	30	18	12			
2	12	− 4	18	14	4			
3	10	− 6	8	8	0			
4	8	− 8	0	0	0	0	0	0
5	6	− 10				10	6	4
6	4	− 12				22	10	12
7	2	− 14				36	12	24
8	0	− 16				52	12	40
9	− 2	− 18				70	10	60
10	− 4	− 20				90	6	84
11	− 6	− 22				112	0	112

damage inflicted upon the neighborhood (column 6) makes one point obvious: If the factory owner is not allowed to harm others, he himself will be harmed. In Coase's view therefore, the problem is a *reciprocal* one, and on efficiency grounds the solution is not simply to restrain the damaging party, but to restrain *either* the damaging *or* the damaged party in such a way that the gain for one side cannot be outweighed by the loss to the other, in total and at the margin.[21] Other than some flawless public policy, what constraints will yield this result?

Let us call the factory owner A and assume the presence of a single neighbor, B. Consider first, as Coase did, what would appear to most of us as a reasonable situation: that Neighbor B has the right to *exclude* pollution so that A will be liable for any damage inflicted on B. In other words, B has an exclusive right to clean air. To calculate the *maximum* amounts A is willing to pay B for the damage at different quantities of input, we must first specify the quantity of input A intends to use. Suppose he intends to operate at four units of input, which generates the maximum social gain. If A's use of input were initially restricted to zero, he would be willing to pay B a maximum of £44 to use four units of input (the sum of £14 + £12 + £10 + £8 in column 4, or A's total private gain). Any requirement that A compensate B with a larger amount would result in no production at all. Similarly, if A's input were initially restricted to one unit, he would be willing to pay B a maximum of £30 to increase that to four units, and so on. These maximums which A would be willing to pay B for the right to use four units of input are listed in column 14. (Any calculation beyond the fourth unit is omitted as irrelevant for decision making.) The *minimums* which B would willingly accept from A as recompense are calculated similarly, except that the marginal values used are now those from column 6. These minimums which will barely compensate B for the damage are shown in column 15.

Any compensation made is a transaction, entailing a contractual agreement between A and B for the use of a stipulated level of input at a mutually agreed term of payment. When A compensates B, he pays for the privilege, or the right, to use resources in certain ways, just as when one buys a house he is

[21]Coase, "The Problem of Social Cost," p. 2.

buying the right to use it in certain ways. A prerequisite for the consummation of any transaction is that the maximum one party is willing to pay to acquire a right is more than, or at least equal to, the minimum another party is willing to accept to surrender that right. As shown in columns 14 and 15, this prerequisite is satisfied for all quantities of input within four units, which means that if A's use of input is at zero, one, or two units, there will be gain from further transacting.[22] The gains from transacting (contracting) at different quantities of input as listed in column 16 are merely the differences between columns 14 and 15. (These gains will necessarily be lower if the use of input intended by A differs less from four units.) If the transaction can be made and enforced without cost, the gain in each case can be shared wholly between A and B, and the postulate of maximization dictates that four units of input will be the chosen quantity for production. Thus far, we see that maximum social gain will be attained under the two constraints that (1) B has the right to exclude any damage by A, and (2) all costs of making the transaction are zero.

It would appear "unreasonable" to most people that the factory owner, A, has a right to inflict damage on B. Yet it is no more "unreasonable" than the earlier example. Instead of A having to pay B for the right to use resources in certain ways, B would now have to pay A for the right to use resources in certain ways, that is, to use his property resource with a lower amount of pollution. The assignment of rights in the two situations will result in different wealth distributions, and what is "fair" to one party is always "unfair" to the other.

By a method analogous to our earlier calculation of values (columns 14 and 15), we obtain in column 17 the *maximum* amounts B is willing to pay A to curtail the use of input, and in column 18 the *minimum* A is willing to accept for that curtailment. Here, however, the relevant range to consider is the use of inputs *beyond* the fourth unit. To illustrate, suppose that to maximize his private gain A chooses to operate at eight units. In view of A's right to inflict damage, B is willing to pay A to

---

[22]Owing to the use of discrete values, three or four units of input yield the same gains. We choose the fourth unit to illustrate the attainment of maximum social gain because the marginal values come to a balance here. Similar confusions exist in our earlier illustrations.

curtail his use of input to four units a maximum of £52 (column 17), which is the sum of £16 + £14 + £12 + £10 (column 6 omitting signs). On the other hand, the *minimum* amount A is willing to accept to limit his use of input to four units is £12, which is the sum of £6 + £4 + £2 (column 4). As shown in columns 17 and 18, the maximum amounts one party is willing to pay at different quantities of inputs again exceed the minimum amounts the other party is willing to accept; and again, in the absence of transaction costs, the gains from contracting at different quantities of input are the largest if input is adjusted to four units. The gains from contracting at varying levels of inputs are once more the difference between the two columns, and these are shown in column 19. Note that in combining columns 16 and 19, we get column 9 in table A, the total values of social economic waste. What would have been wasted now becomes gains from contracting.

A more general statement can now be made regarding the constraints under which the traditional measure of economic efficiency will be attained. First, assignment of exclusive rights to *either* A *or* B is essential, and either case will yield similar results. (The alternative assignments of rights, involving alternative liability rules and different distributions of wealth, could lead to different patterns of resource use due to the distribution effects, but this would not affect efficiency.) A second constraint is that all costs associated with making transactions are zero. These two propositions summarize what has been called the Coase theorem.

<hr>

COMPLICATIONS
*[This section can be skipped by noneconomists—*ED.*]*

Complication 1: Uncertain transaction costs

This illustration gives rise to several important complications which should be examined, to clarify our understanding of social cost and to facilitate subsequent discussion of the appropriate specification of constraints. To demonstrate the first complication, return to the situation where Neighbor B has the right to exclude damage by Factory Owner A. We have discovered that the total gain of increasing input from zero to four units is £24 (column 16), but how is this gain to be divided between A and B? No matter how it is apportioned, assuming transaction costs to be zero, four units of input will be employed. But this result merely follows *tautologically* from the postulate of constrained maximization. How can there be any other outcome if all parties are able to maximize by contracting without cost to them? The question of division of the gain must first be solved. Either party *may* capture the entire amount; but no criterion or mechanism is specified through which a division may be determined, and without an answer to this question we cannot predict the behavior of the individual parties.

Bilateral monopoly

The problem here is identical to that of a monopolist (single seller) dealing with a monopsonist (single buyer): The solution has long been regarded as indeterminate. Economic theory fails to yield any definitive implications because the constraints are inadequately specified. In such a bilateral monopoly, the transaction costs are significant because of a lack of competitive forces to reduce them. To assume away such costs, therefore, is to commit the same fallacy which this section is designed to correct. Yet to say that transaction costs are significant is again saying very little; we need to know also their magnitude and nature. The mere recognition that transaction costs affect behavior will not contribute much to interpret it; what is important is an understanding of the factors which determine the transaction costs. In other words, if transaction costs are significant for the problem at hand and must be specified as part of the constraints, it is imperative that we evaluate these costs under different circumstances, or no testable implications can be derived.

Suppose Neighbor B has the right to exclude damage, but his property happens to be in a location with special advantages for shoe production, and that a large number of shoe producers similar to A are willing to bid for it. B is thus a monopolist but A is a competitive buyer of location. Transaction costs have been reduced, because competition has generated offers to B from prospective shoe producers. Other details such as the physical attributes of the damaging effects, the forms of contract enforceable in the courts, and so on, may indicate that the transaction costs are so low that they have little significance in determining the division of the gain and so can be ignored with much gain in simplicity. The highest competing offer made to B for the use of four units of input will then be £44 (column 14), which means that Monopolist B will capture the entire gain of £24.

Suppose now that B, too, must compete with owners in other locations. If transaction costs are ignored, the "price taker" situation emerges. Contracting for the use of four units of inputs, A will pay B £8 per unit of input use, an amount equal to the value of the marginal damage. The total payment from A to B is £32 which, deducting a total of £20 for damage suffered by B, yields him a gain of £12. The gain of £12 is, coincidentally, half of the total social gain of £24—the remaining half goes to A. The abstraction from transaction costs is proper only if they are ascertained to be insignificant. Otherwise, the total gain will be less than £24 and its division will differ. The important conclusion is that the *solution becomes mechanical once the nature and magnitude of transaction costs, together with other constraints, are sufficiently specified.*

Complication 2: High transaction costs

A second complication is that transaction costs may be so high that they preclude transaction. This may happen if the effects imposed by one individual on another require too costly measurement, or if they affect a multitude concurrently and in a way which imposes a high cost in dividing or sharing the compensation. The values in table D then display interesting results. If Neighbor B has the right to exclude damage and thereby restrains A's use of input to zero, the total loss to society will be £24 (column 16). On the other hand, if A has the right to inflict damage, in the absence of any payment by B he will employ eight units of input (to maximize private gain), and the loss to society will be £40 (column 19). On efficiency grounds, therefore, A should be denied the right to inflict damage. In other words, if transaction costs are prohibitive or even sizable, *the arbitrary assignment of rights influences the use of resources and the gain to society.*[23]

Suppose that the costs of contracting for the use of four units of input are the same under alternative assignments of rights. If these transaction costs are less than £24, assignment of property rights to either A or B will result in contracting.[24] If, however, these costs are higher than £24 but less than £40, a contract will be obtained if A has the right to inflict damage but not if B has the right to exclude damage. Such a contract will cost more than £24 and will therefore be more wasteful to society than the absence of a contract resulting from the assignment of rights to B. *The mere attainment of a contract, therefore, is not a priori evidence of a move toward more efficient use of resources; conversely, the absence of contracting may enhance efficiency.*

If transaction costs are prohibitive, the government may step in with corrective policies to regulate the use of inputs to four units whilst incurring administrative costs of less than £24. In this case Pigou's original conclusion holds, though supported by a different analysis. On the other hand, the government may step in even if the administrative costs of intervention are higher than £24 or £40, whereas, had these been private transaction costs, no contract would have been reached. Behavior differs because policy makers and private in-

[23]This point is recognized by Coase (p. 16).
[24]With positive transaction costs, different forms of contracts may affect resource allocation in different ways; hence contracting may or may not imply the use of four units of input in our illustration. This complication is very important but a fuller elaboration is beyond the scope of this paper.

dividuals confront different constraints, and their options of choice differ accordingly. Indeed, even if the costs of private contracting were insignificant, a government might still decide to intervene. Economic analysis has thus far failed to predict the circumstances under which government action will incur lower (or higher) costs than those resulting from private contracting.

Complication 3: Absence of diminishing returns

Consider a third complication. The law of diminishing returns may not hold in a situation where marginal uncontracted effects (column 6) are negative: Instead of rising in absolute terms as input increases, this value may become zero at some level of input and remain zero thereafter. In a court case cited by Coase,[25] the construction of a tall building casts a shadow over a swimming pool nearby. After the building reaches a certain height, its further elevation may do little or no harm. Similarly, a residential apartment which has declined in value as a result of a polluting factory nearby may at some point be converted into a warehouse to halt the loss in property value.

Suppose the marginal damage is reduced to zero at the third unit of input and thereafter (table D). The total possible damage inflicted by A is £6 (the absolute sum of the first three values in column 6). However, maximum social gain is here attained at eight units of input, where the total private gain of £56 (the sum of the first eight values in column 4) exceeds the total damage (£6) by a total social gain of £50. If transaction costs are zero, contracting between A and B will lead to the use of eight units of input regardless of who holds the exclusive right. If such costs are prohibitive, granting A the right to inflict damage will lead to the use of eight units of input, whereas granting B the right to exclude damage will result in no input and a social waste of £50. Finally, if the transaction costs are not prohibitive, granting A the right will lead to no contracting and the use of eight units of input, whereas granting B the right to exclude damage will lead to contracting for the use of the same input but at a social waste of the transaction costs incurred. This complication demonstrates not only that alternative assignments of rights may affect resource allocation when the transaction costs are positive, but also that the *transaction costs incurred may vary with alternative assignments of rights.*

Complication 4: Unlimited property rights/ prohibitive transaction costs

Consider finally a fourth complication. Suppose A has the right to inflict damage on B. It may be recalled that in maximizing his own gain A will employ eight units of input. But why only eight units? In

[25]Coase, p. 8.

deliberately employing *more* units of input and thereby *losing* from the marginal sale of shoes (column 4), A may be able to extort a payment from B (see column 17) which more than compensates his self-inflicted loss.[26] It now becomes clear that one must qualify what was taken as a foregone conclusion in the Pigovian tradition—that private gain will necessarily be maximized at eight units of input. One set of constraints which supports such a conclusion includes not only A's right to inflict damage on B, but also the existence of prohibitive transaction costs.

Granting exclusive property rights implies setting limits within which the individual may exercise them so as to generate income. In the right to use a resource, these limits may refer to (i) a limited number of ways to use the resource, such as the right to inflict or to exclude damage; or (ii) a limited magnitude within which a right may be exercised, such as restricting pollution to a stated amount. The latter limitation may be set by the physical attributes of the resources (as with the building which overshadows the pool), by legal or customary constraints, or by such private arrangements as mutual agreement on the use of four units of input. Indeed, some mutually agreed limits are implicit in every contract, together with a delimitation of rights as defined by laws, custom, and physical attributes.

Economists following Pigou (but not Pigou himself) have primarily concerned themselves with corrective legal devices to restrain the second type of limits on rights; and their misspecification of constraints (including that by Pigou himself) leaves a good deal to be desired in their analyses. Today, an increasing number of economists have broadened their outlook on contracting; yet most still consider the first class of limits (the alternative assignment of rights) as beyond the scope of private agreements. To see the error of this view, one need only examine a broad spectrum of existing private contracts.[27] No hard line separates limitations of rights which are matters of *private* contracting from those which fall within the jurisdiction of the court or the coercion of *government*. (Indeed, the very definition of "government" is itself still subject to debate and conjecture.) But whatever government is, its economic role in society must remain unclear until we can pinpoint the activities where governmental intervention incurs lower costs than private contracting.

[26]Indeed Producer A may at relatively low cost adopt special devices which generate more pollution, or he may merely threaten to do so in his attempt to attain a higher income.

[27]A general discussion of the role of contracting is in Steven N. S. Cheung, "The Structure of a Contract and the Theory of a Non-exclusive Resource," *Journal of Law and Economics,* April 1970, pp. 49–70. A recent important investigation by John Umbeck shows that all types of rights may be subject to private contracting: "A Theoretical and Empirical Investigation into the Formation of Property Rights: The California Gold Rush" (Ph.D. diss., University of Washington, 1975).

5. The Constraints in Social-Cost Analysis

In specifying the constraints sufficient to yield testable implications for the interpretation of behavior, two requirements must be met. First, the constraints must be identifiable by observation. Thus, any empirically useful definition of property rights must provide observable situations where changes in rights occur. However, a "right" is an abstract legal concept, not observable by itself, and it is generally impossible to envisage the structure of rights governing a resource merely by observing how it is used. Hence, a change in rights can be identified only by inference from changes in some logically related observations. A second requirement, if property rights are to be useful in economic theorizing, is that they be defined in such a way that (given constrained maximization) changes in behavior can be derived as a result of changes of rights.

Degrees of property rights

Any economic good—a house, quietness, or clean air—embodies a set of characteristics with measurable limits in use. The constraints of property rights vary not only when these use limits vary but, more importantly, when the *rights* to these limits vary. A good or an asset is defined to be private property if, and only if, three distinct sets of rights are associated with its ownership. First, the exclusive right to *use* (or to decide how to use) the good may be viewed as the right to exclude other individuals from its use. Second is the exclusive right to receive *income* generated by the use of the good. Third, the full right to *transfer,* or freely "alienate," its ownership includes the right to enter into contracts and to choose their form. This structure of rights which defines private property is, of course, an idealization intended for economic theorizing; in practice, exclusivity and transferability are matters of degree.

However, with definite relationships among the above rights dictated by the postulate of constrained maximization, the idealization permits us to press the implications of other structures of rights which depart from it. Consider first the relationship between the right to use and the right to income. The presence of an exclusive-use right does not imply an exclusive right to derive income from the use. A landowner who has the right to fence off trespassers may be partly or wholly denied rental income from his holding if taxation or price control attenuates his exclusive right to that income. The loss of the exclusive right to receive income will then lead to the same sort of behavior as though his right to use were not exclusive. No maximizing individual will exercise his right to exclusive use of a resource if he cannot derive any exclusive income from that effort.[28]

Exclusive right to a resource, moreover, does not imply that its ownership is transferable. A college professor granted exclusive rights to his office is not usually entitled to lease it to another. But transferability does imply that the resource is, at least to some degree, exclusively owned. No maximizing individual will agree on stipulations in a contract governing the use of a resource, or the terms for its payment, if the rights to its use or to its income are not exclusive.

If behavior is to be interpreted in terms of economic principles, the most basic requirement is that we be able to identify any changing pattern of these rights so that implications can be derived for corresponding changes in contractual behavior, resource allocation, and income distribution. The rights governing a resource cannot be identified merely by observing its use; nor are the rights themselves observable. How are we to infer from different situations the corresponding changes in rights? The lack of exclusive property rights may be attributed to their nonrecognition by legal or social institutions, or to prohibitively high costs of delineating and policing their limits. Similarly, the transfer of rights in the market is also constrained by institutions and by the costs of negotiating and enforcing contracts. In drawing inferences on changes in rights

[28]A fuller discussion (and about circumstances where the right to receive income is partially attenuated) is in Steven N. S. Cheung, "A Theory of Price Control," *Journal of Law and Economics,* March 1974, pp. 53–71.

through observable institutional changes or changes in the costs of transacting, we are confronted with the problem of inseparable costs.

Defining the scope of transaction costs

In the broadest sense of the term, "transaction costs" comprise those that cannot be conceived to exist in a Crusoe economy. The term then includes not only the costs of forming and enforcing contracts (including seeking information for market transactions), but also the costs of delineating and policing exclusive rights (including those of institutional arrangements such as legislative enactments). This wide definition is essential, for it is difficult (and, insofar as we know, impossible) to separate the cost of exchange from the cost of defining rights to the resource to be exchanged.

On the one hand, the income derivable from an exclusive right, or the *gain* of enforcing it, depends on transferability in the marketplace, for otherwise the highest valued option may not be realized. The lower the costs of contracting for transfer, the higher therefore will be the gain of enforcing exclusivity. Conversely, the *cost* of enforcing exclusivity also depends on the availability of transfer and on its associated costs. Thus, where exclusion costs vary with the size of a resource holding, low transfer costs permit holdings to be rearranged so as to reduce exclusion costs. The problem posed by this inseparability of costs resembles that found with products produced jointly by the same inputs. In either situation, however, implications for hypotheses and tests may be derived if we are able to specify the *marginal* variations of particular (transaction) costs under different circumstances.

Under the preceding broad definition of transaction costs, and accepting the conclusion of the Coase theorem, to say that transaction costs are zero is identical to declaring the existence of *private* property rights (as defined earlier in this section).[29] In principle, therefore, it is possible to specify the constraints of transaction costs in such a comprehensive way that they encompass all the constraints of property rights. In practice,

[29]Strictly interpreted, the Coase theorem requires the presence either of private property rights *or* of zero transaction costs, not both.

however, such specification will be unnecessarily complex. One general rule for simplification is to treat as variables constraints subject to the discretion of the individual whose behavior we seek to explain, and to take as given other relevant constraints beyond his control. To analyze an individual's behavior in installing a lock to his home, we treat the cost of the installation as a variable (since he can choose among locks at different costs) while taking the existing police force as given and ignoring the cost of police protection (to which the citizen has contributed through taxation but the amount of which is beyond his control). It is therefore generally advisable to treat the constraints established by legal or social institutions separately from the costs of forming and enforcing private contracts, which are only part of transaction costs in a broader sense.

Observing property rights via a study of constraints

Depending, then, on the observation we seek to explain and on the availability of information, inferences about changes in the three types of rights may be drawn from investigating the institutional constraints, the constraints of transaction costs, or both. An alteration of rights effected by law may be identified not only by the observed changes in law itself, but also by the efforts devoted to enforcing it. (Thus, a careful specification of legal constraints may require the examination of an enormous number of court cases.) Similarly, with respect to transaction costs, refutable implications can be obtained if we are able to identify one certain observable situation which entails higher or lower costs, in total and at the margin, than another. Furthermore, it is not necessary that transaction costs under different situations be actually *measured: Ranking* these costs in different circumstances will often suffice. With such a ranking, the test of any implication derived from it will also serve as a test of the ranking itself, and the validity of the ranking will be enhanced by the presence and confirmation of multiple-test implications. A more useful method, of course, is to propose generalized functions of transaction costs which may be systematically applied to a larger number of situations. This task is onerous, as the current state of the art amply demonstrates.

6. Fallacies in the
Reporting of Observations

The development of an empirical science may be judged by one criterion: What fraction of its hypotheses has been tested against hard evidence? By this measure economics would fail. In few other empirical sciences are the practitioners so willing to accept theorems or so reluctant to test the alternative implications of their hypotheses. Such behavior is compounded by the often casual attitude of economists towards the authentication of their "facts," particularly in social cost.

Using imaginary "facts" to support imaginary policies seems habitual in the Pigovian tradition. It would be extremely costly to assess the general reliability of the real-world examples cited to justify corrective actions by government. To my knowledge, however, not a single popular example has been supported by hard evidence. In some cases divergence can be shown between private and social cost by its traditional measure. The issue is not divergence itself, but the reliability of the observations used to illustrate it. If to a significant extent these observations are untrue, economists have tried to explain things which do not exist and have formulated policies largely inappropriate for application.

Divergences between Private and Social Costs:
Two Empirical Investigations

(I) EFFECTS OF LAND TENURE ON AGRICULTURAL EFFICIENCY

I have investigated two widely accepted examples alleged to exhibit divergences between private and social costs: land tenure in agriculture, and apples and bees. Pigou devoted more space to land tenure than to any other example in his discussion of social cost.[30] In his view, tenant cultivation is generally less efficient than owner cultivation owing to defects found in tenure contracts. These defects may stem from actions which generate beneficial effects, such as improvements on land made by a tenant:

> It is true that a tenant can claim compensation [from his landlord] for improvements on quitting. But he knows that the rent may be raised against him on the strength of his improvements, and his compensation claim does not come into force unless he takes the extreme step of giving up the farm.[31]

Alternatively, the actions may be harmful, such as depletion of the soil by the tenant:

> Indeed, it is often found that, towards the close of his tenancy, a farmer, in the natural and undisguised endeavour to get back as much of his capital as possible, takes so much out of the land that, for some years afterwards, the yield is markedly reduced.[32]

Pigou went on the discuss compensation schemes recognized by law, their shortcomings, and additional corrective policies.

Having quarrelled elsewhere with the argument in general,[33] I do not here attack Pigou's logic. Although in varying details the assertion of economic inefficiency in tenant cultivation can be dated at least as early as Adam Smith, Pigou brought the focus to bear on social cost. What I challenge here is the accuracy of the "facts" asserted by Pigou. Using the library facilities of the University of Chicago, I checked his evidence, seeking out the sources he cited, the references cited in them, and so on, until I could go no further. *No* evidence of inefficient tenant farming was discovered.

Requirements in testing Pigou's claim

Anyone seeking to support or refute Pigou's claim of defective contracting in agriculture must meet two requirements. First, the constraints governing agricultural resources in the

---

[30]*Economics of Welfare,* pp. 150–59.

[31]Ibid., p. 156.

[32]Ibid., p. 151.

[33]Steven N. S. Cheung, *The Theory of Share Tenancy* (Chicago: University of Chicago Press, 1969).

period and location where the data are gathered must conform in essential aspects to those underlying Pigou's argument; second, reliable and relevant data must be available. Implicit in Pigou's argument is that private ownership governs agricultural resources. "Private ownership" here does not refer to the idealized structure of private property rights discussed in section 5, but rather to

(1) private title to agricultural resources;
(2) exclusivity and transferability of these resources, in some degree enforced by institutions;
(3) a positive, but not prohibitive, cost in contracting; and
(4) the absence of regulations severely restraining market activities.

In view of (4), the use of postwar data is precluded in many countries by land reform, farm support, and price control policies. On the other hand, agricultural data are scarce for the prewar period. To select a period and a location with the required constraints and data, prewar China seems to be the best choice.

Farmers refute Pigou

In the 1920s and early 1930s in China, arguments against tenant farming were common, and the desirability of private land-ownership was frequently debated. Lacking disciplined economic analysis to support their arguments, several Chinese organizations and independent writers resorted to empirical investigations ended in 1935 by the Sino-Japanese War. But their findings, incorporated by a monumental effort of Professor J. L. Buck, constituted the most comprehensive body of evidence relating to agricultural land use under unregulated private property rights that I could find.[34] Data gathered without the

---

[34]Under the auspices of the University of Nanking, Buck directed a forty-man team in the compilation of farming data in China during 1929–36. The original data, which appear to have passed unnoticed, are available in J. L. Buck, ed., *Land Utilization in China—Statistics—A Study of 16,786 Farms in 168 Localities and 38,256 Farm Families in Twenty-two Provinces in China, 1929–1933* (Nanking: University of Nanking, 1937). During the preparation of this impressive volume, Buck wrote the noted *Chinese Farm Economy* (1930), and *Land Utilization in China* (1937), both of which have been distributed by the University of Chicago Press. However, Buck's earlier works are also important: *An Economic and Social Survey of 102 Farms near Wuhu, Anhwoi, China* (Nanking, 1923); *An Economic and Social Survey of 150 Farms,*

aid of a definite hypothesis tend to include much irrelevant material. For our present purpose, however, the tests we seek to perform do not require a high level of sophistication, and the findings in China are so comprehensive as to permit several crucial tests of Pigou's argument. The data gathered by separate sources are generally consistent with one another, which is remarkable considering that the findings encompass twenty-two provinces in China over a period of fifteen years.

(a) The first implication of Pigou's argument is that the yields in tenant farms will be significantly lower than in owner farms. But as Buck observed (China, 1921–25):

> Contrary to the prevailing opinion that tenants do not farm as well as owners, a classification according to yields by different types of tenure shows no significant variation in yields for most localities, and for the few in which a difference does occur, it is in favour of the tenant or part-owner as often as for the owner....In some places, even, it is evident that the tenants farm better than the owners.[35]

Buck's data show the following crop indexes per acre: owner farms, 100 and 101; part-owner farms, 99 and 101; and tenant farms, 103 and 104.[36] Similarly, adjusted for fertility grades and locations, "the value of land for the three types of tenure (owner, part-owner, and tenant) in most cases varies only a few dollars."[37]

(b) A second implication of Pigou's argument is that agricultural productivity under tenant cultivation will vary according to the duration of the lease: namely, the shorter the lease the less productive the farming. This in turn implies that

---

Yehshan County, Hopei, China (Nanking, 1926); and *Farm Ownership and Tenancy in China* (Shanghai: National Christian Council, 1927).

Surveys by independent writers aside, others have been conducted by organizations, including the Department of Internal Affairs, the Real Estate Bureau, the National Government Statistics Department, the Executive Yuan, and the Legislative Yuan.

[35]Buck, *Chinese Farm Economy,* pp. 156–57.

[36]Ibid. Buck's finding is from a sample of 2,542 farms in fifteen localities, seven provinces, China. The slightly higher yields per acre in tenant farms are perhaps due to a higher proportion of paddy fields under tenancy, which Buck did not discern. Similar evidence is in Buck, *Farm Ownership and Tenancy in China.*

[37]Buck, *Chinese Farm Economy,* p. 156.

the shorter the lease, other things equal, the lower the rental value of land. An investigation (1934) covering a total of ninety-three prefectures in eight Chinese provinces showed that the distribution of lease duration was as follows:

29 percent of the tenant leases *indefinite* (that is, unspecified and usually terminable after every harvest);

25 percent *annual* leases;

27 percent from *3 to 10 years;*

8 percent from *10 to 20 years;* and

11 percent *perpetual* leases.[38]

This distribution shows such a large variation that if lease duration is a significant determinant of productivity, it will be revealed in the rental data. Yet in three separate surveys (China, 1930, 1932, and 1936), the data show that in twenty-two provinces the rental values vary mainly with land grades[39] and that share-rent contracts, which generally have shorter lease durations than fixed-rent contracts, yield slightly higher rental values than do fixed rents.[40]

(c) A third implication of Pigou's argument is that nonland inputs committed to farming, including improvements made on land, are less on tenant farms than on owner farms. Again the falsifying evidence is strong. Two indepedent surveys (China, 1921–24 and 1935) revealed that on tenant farms landowners owned about 60 to 70 percent of the housing assets while tenants owned about 75 percent of the draft animals and 95 percent of the farming equipment. Except for the value of housing (higher on owner farms), these surveys show roughly the same total values of nonland assets on owner as on tenant farms.[41] Not only were permanent improvements routinely stipulated in tenant contracts, but enforcement efforts by landlords were also evident.[42] Indeed, the kinds of activities

---

[38]These percentages are calculated from data in Department of Real Estates, *China Economic Yearbook, 1935,* pp. 101–4.

[39]Department of Internal Affairs, *Public Reports of Internal Affairs,* 2, vols. 1 and 2 (1932). See also Legislative Yuan, *Statistical Monthly,* 2.5 (1930).

[40]Department of Real Estates, *China Economic Yearbook, 1936,* pp. G62–83.

[41]National Government, Statistics Department, *Statistical Analysis in Tenancy System in China* (1942), pp. 99–116.

[42]Cf. Pe-Yu Chang and Yin-Yuen Wang, *Questions of Farm Tenancy in China* (1943), p. 49; also Ching-Moh Chen, *Land Rents of Various Provinces in*

which Pigou visualized as defectively contracted, or beyond the scope of private contracting, are precisely the activities stated in every written contract that I could find.[43] Moreover, the compensation schemes which Pigou proposed to legislate were incorporated in the adjustments of rental payments:

> The percentage of total receipts for the landlord varies from 24.7 per cent,...where small rents are demanded to 66.6 per cent,...where the cropper system prevails and where the landlord furnishes everything but labour and routine management.[44]

Similarly, according to another survey conducted in four provinces (China, 1934), an average rental percentage of 55.98 was found on tenant farms where landlords provided seeds, fertilizers, and bullocks, as compared to an average of 46.37 percent where the tenants provided these nonland inputs.[45]

The evidence thus disputes Pigou's claim of inefficient tenant farming. Although private and social costs may yet diverge in tenant farming, the Chinese experience indicates that it is not in any of the forms Pigou claimed. This is not to say that the "deficient" tenure arrangements which he asserted may not have existed in the locations of his reference. But if they did, the constraints governing farming and contractual decisions in those locations must have conformed neither to those in China (1921–35) nor, according to my interpretation, to those Pigou implicitly employed in his analysis. In other words, Pigou has erred either in reporting the observations or in specifying the constraints.

The lack of significant variation between owner and tenant cultivation in the data presented does not imply that the costs of negotiating and enforcing tenant contracts in China or elsewhere are trivial, or that they will not affect observations in

China (1936); Chi-Ming Chiao, *A Social and Economic Study of Farm Villages in China* (1938); and China Economic Research Department, *Source Materials of Recent Chinese Agricultural History* (1957), pp. 89–95.

[43]Sample tenancy contracts can be found in National Government, *Statistical Analysis in Tenancy System in China,* p. 54; and Chang and Wang, *Questions of Farm Tenancy in China,* pp. 63–64.

[44]Buck, *Chinese Farm Economy,* p. 149. The rental shares provided are averages of sample farms in eleven localities in China (1921–25), and the 66.6 percent cited is purely incidental.

[45]These averages are calculated from Chen, *Land Rents,* pp. 102–3.

some decisive ways. But, while recognizing these transaction costs, we must not jump to the conclusion that tenant farming will be less productive than owner farming. Whether transaction costs will significantly affect behavior depends upon their impact on resource use *at the margin*. With or without such costs, maximization may imply the same *marginal* equality: Namely, for the use of crucial farming resources the marginal return to the input committed equals its marginal opportunity cost. If so, the data on resource use will exhibit little variation among different tenure arrangements. It is true that transaction costs incurred are generally higher with tenant than with owner cultivation, but there is no reason to predict that they are of such proportion or nature that they significantly affect resource use at the crucial margin. Under the constraints of private property rights in agriculture, transaction costs chiefly affect the choice of alternative tenure arrangements.[46] Furthermore, given the portfolios of farming assets chosen by individuals, the gains from tenant farming must, by definition, have exceeded the increases in transaction costs when some of the assets were contracted out.

(II) THE CASE OF THE APPLES AND THE BEES

When Professor J. E. Meade introduced the widely accepted example of divergence between private and social costs in apple farming and beekeeping, it was not clear whether he used it as a factual case or only allegorically to illustrate some theoretical points.[47] Yet my impression from reading the subsequent literature and from talking to economists is that this example has been taken at face value. Meade refers to "the case of an unpaid factor, because the situation is due simply and solely to the fact that the apple-farmer cannot charge the beekeeper for the bees' food..."[48] The "underproduction" of apples as a result calls for subsidization of apple farming. Moreover, the

---

[46]Steven N. S. Cheung, "Transaction Costs, Risk Aversion, and the Choice of Contractual Arrangements," *Journal of Law and Economics,* April 1969, pp. 23–42.

[47]Meade, "External Economies and Diseconomies."

[48]Ibid., p. 57.

"unpaid factor" may be of a reciprocal nature, and this would call for not only subsidies but also taxes:

> While the apples may provide the food of the bees, the bees may fertilise the apples....we can obtain formulae to show what subsidies and taxes must be imposed....[49]

Beekeepers refute Meade

In 1972 I conducted a field investigation in the State of Washington, one of the largest apple-growing areas in the world. Refutation of Meade's "unpaid factor" was provided by the contractual arrangements that have long been routine between farmers and beekeepers. But to clarify the observations on pricing and contractual behavior, my investigation included a study of the physical and biological aspects of bees and of the related flowering plants, and covered a sample of nine Washington beekeepers managing around ten thousand colonies and serving approximately two hundred farms. The data were drawn primarily from apiary and pollination contracts, from the accounting records of beekeepers, and from conversations with beekeepers and farmers. Contrary to what most of us have thought, apple blossoms yield little or no honey. But it is true that bees provide valuable pollination services for apples and other plants, and that many other plants yield lucrative honey crops. Thus a major effort was directed to investigate the varied volumes of nectar flows and pollination requirements of plants.

Introducing the analysis of the observed pricing behavior, I wrote:

> It is easy to find conclusive evidence showing that *both nectar and pollination services are transacted in the market-place:* in some cities one need look no further than the yellow pages of the Telephone Directory. But the existence of prices does not in itself confirm efficient allocation of resources.
>
> It is, therefore, necessary to demonstrate the effectiveness of the market in dictating the use of even those resources—bees, nectar, and pollen—which, admittedly, are elusive in character and relatively insignificant in value....I shall not attempt to estimate the standard sets of marginal values which an efficient market is said to

[49]Ibid., p. 58.

equate: *the burden of such a task must rest upon those who believe the government can costlessly and accurately make these estimates for the imposition of the "ideal" tax-subsidy schemes.* Rather, I offer below an analysis based on the equimarginal principle. To the extent that the observed pricing and contractual behaviour fails to falsify the implications derived from this analysis we conclude that (1) the observed behaviour is explained, and (2) the observations are consistent with efficient allocation of resources.[50] (Italics added.)

To this end, a theoretical analysis was made of the reciprocal process in which a beekeeper is able to extract honey from the farm to which he renders pollination service. The polar cases were also analyzed: where bees are employed only for the extraction of honey or only for pollination. The analysis treated pollination services and honey yield simply as components of a joint product generated by the hive. That is, the rental price per hive received by a beekeeper for placing his hives on a farm may be paid in (a) honey (which may be positive or negative), or (b) a money fee (always positive if only for pollination service and always negative—an apiary rent paid *to* the farm owner—if only for honey extraction), or (c) a combination of these. The value of the marginal product of a hive is the aggregate of the marginal nectar product and the marginal pollination product. Under competition, the value of the marginal product of a hive will be the same on every farm and, in turn, will equal the rental price per hive and the marginal (opportunity) cost of producing and keeping the hive. The statistical results supporting this analysis are in a Note at the end of this section (p. 49).

Costs of information and government action

The investigation of beekeeping vis à vis farming reveals another weakness in the traditional argument for corrective government actions. The resources employed in pollination and nectar extraction are insignificant in value and, given that farmers could easily keep bees themselves, the gain from contracting with specialist beekeepers is trivial. Some farmers, par-

---

[50]Steven N. S. Cheung, "The Fable of the Bees: An Economic Investigation," *Journal of Law and Economics,* April 1973, p. 19.

ticularly on larger farms, keep bees themselves. But suppose that, instead of private contracting, the government were to introduce tax-subsidy schemes to regulate beekeeping and farming. To calculate the proper rates of such "ideal" schemes requires knowledge of the marginal value of honey and pollination. Entomologists would testify that to obtain this knowledge would require repetitive and costly experiments. To develop a reliable estimate of the marginal schedules of even one type of farm is costly. In the State of Washington alone, twenty or thirty types of farms differ sufficiently so that each might call for a specially tailored scheme of tax or subsidy. Casual empiricism suggests that in beekeeping and farming the *cost* of devising these schemes, let alone the cost of administering them, would *exceed* the contracting gain many times.

Would it be equally costly to determine the schedules of the marginal values under *private* contracting? The answer is that *the market does not require this knowledge in directing resource allocation.* As a businessman, the farmer is continuously experimenting, imitating others, and constantly seeking ways to increase his wealth. Counting money in alternative situations may alone generate sufficient information for his purpose. The equimarginal principle may be totally irrelevant to his decision making, and knowledge of the schedules of marginal productivities may be as unnecessary to him as knowledge about the chemical formula of his soil.

What he requires for making money bears absolutely no relation to what is required by the economist who theorizes about *why* the farmer behaves as he does. The equimarginal principle is a tool, invented for that purpose by the economist, to mesh observable changes in constraints into gear with observable changes in behavior, so that "constrained maximization" becomes formally operative. No part of this paradigm requires that marginal schedules should themselves be observed, or that individual decisions be based on knowledge of them.

Therefore, to evaluate the usefulness of the theory, the criterion is not the reality of the marginal schedules, but whether the implications we derive from it are testable and confirmed by evidence. And to evaluate the success of the farmer or the beekeeper (or any entrepreneur), *the criterion is not his knowledge of the marginal values, but whether he makes enough money to survive in business.*[51] The wealth of an entrepreneur is part of society's wealth; thus any private decision error which results in a loss in wealth imposes a cost on society. In the contractual employment of bees, the contracting costs include those of forming the contracts and of whatever losses may derive from erroneous contractual decisions. Since the gains from such contracting are trivial, the contracting costs are, by definition, even more insignificant.

The situation is very different if private contracting is to be replaced by tax-subsidy policies. Since the constraints on government decisions differ from those on private parties, the options of choice also differ. In government activity, making a pound more or a pound less no longer serves the same guidelines as in private decision making. The government, too, may count pounds in different situations, but, now that no one has an exclusive right to the money, this counting will not be based on the same incentive as for private gain. In other words, counting pounds for keeps is frequently the *least costly* method to obtain information for wealth-maximizing decisions, a method uniquely consistent with the constraints of private property rights. If this method of obtaining information is not used, devising "ideal" tax-subsidy schemes, in the example of farming and beekeeping, requires government to assess the marginal-value schedules.

The costs of private contracting are not always and necessarily lower than the costs of deriving and enforcing public policies to achieve the same end. What is true of the bees should not be generalized to all other economic activities. Indeed, it is safe to assert that governments do not exist without economic reasons, although again no convincing analysis has identified the kind of activities for which the government enjoys cost advantages over the market. But any government action can be speciously justified on efficiency grounds by the simple expedient of assuming that transaction costs in the market are high and that costs of governmental control are low. The use of such arbitrary (often implicit) assumptions, a routine practice in the traditional analysis of social cost, is ap-

[51]Armen A. Alchian, "Uncertainty, Evolution and Economic Theory," *Journal of Political Economy,* June 1950, pp. 211-21.

propriate neither for economic explanation nor for policy formulation.

Economists' imagination and the real world

In land tenure and in the activity of bees the alleged deficiencies of market arrangements are not supported by the evidence. Henry Sidgwick's classic example of the lighthouse as a public good from which users who will not pay cannot be excluded has recently been opened to question.[52] Similarly, I contend that problems of environmental degradation diverge in essential aspects from what economists seem to believe. Even a close look into various forms of real-property transactions confirms that such factors as barking dogs and crying babies are duly considered in rental contracts for apartments, and that cleanliness and quietness are routinely valued in pricing. The charges laid at the door of economists for their cavalier attitude toward the facts are not insignificant, as I conclude in my study of the bees:

> I have no grounds for criticizing Meade and other economists who follow the Pigovian tradition for their use of the bee example to illustrate a theoretical point: certainly, resource allocation would in general differ from what is observed if the factors were "unpaid". My main criticism, rather, concerns their approach to economic inquiry in failing to investigate the real-world situation and in arriving at policy implications out of sheer imagination. As a result, their work contributes little to our understanding of the actual economic system.[53]

NOTE TO SECTION 6

An Empirical Study of Beehive Rentals

The chief statistical result was drawn from a study of thirteen flowering crops, with varying numbers of beekeepers and farmers taking part in the cultivation of each. Among a number of implications tested, two related ones are particularly important. The first is that the rental price per hive is roughly the same among different uses in different farms, regardless of drastic variation in the nectar flows and the

---

[52] R. H. Coase, "The Lighthouse in Economics," *Journal of Law and Economics,* October 1974, pp. 357–76.

[53] Cheung, "The Fable of the Bees," p. 33.

pollination requirements of the plants. The coefficient of variation of the rental prices of hives used only for pollination services is 0.035. When the computation is extended to include honey extraction, with honey yields converted into monetary terms and added to the pollination fees, the coefficient of variation is 0.042. We may compare these coefficients of variations with those cited by Professor George Stigler:[54] automobile prices (0.017) and anthracite coal prices (0.068). Not only are the "unpaid factors" in practice paid, but also the variation in unit payments under different farming conditions is so slight that the allocation of hives and nectar flows approximates that of a smoothly functioning market.

A second, and more illuminating, implication is that an inverse relationship exists between the pollination fee (hive rental in money) and the expected honey yield (hive rental in kind). Again, the supporting evidence is strong. Letting x_0 be the total rent per hive, x_1 be the rent paid in money, and x_2 be the expected rent paid in nectar,[55] the variance of x_0 is broken down to

$$\sigma^2_{x_0} = \sigma^2_{x_1} + \sigma^2_{x_2} + 2 \text{ Cov } (x_1, x_2).$$

For any particular farm, either x_1 or x_2 may be positive or negative. Since a hive has different alternative values in different seasons, the data for spring and summer are separated. For the spring season, the corresponding values of the above equation are

$$0.166 = 1.620 + 2.317 - 3.771.$$

The coefficient of correlation between x_1 and x_2 is -0.973. For the summer season, the values corresponding to the above equation are

$$0.806 = 5.414 + 6.183 - 10.791.$$

The coefficient of correlation between x_1 and x_2 is -0.933. The testing of other implications, for which I refer the reader to the lengthier paper,[56] further confirms that the value of marginal product per hive, the rental price, and the marginal cost of producing and keeping the hive all tend to be equated.

[54]"The Economics of Information," *Journal of Political Economy,* 1961, p. 213.
[55]That is, $x_0 = x_1 + x_2$. The corresponding values for the spring (chiefly pollination) season are $9.65 = $9.02 + 0.64; the corresponding values for the summer (chiefly honey) season are $8.07 = $1.30 + 6.77.
[56]Cheung, "The Fable of the Bees."

7. Conclusion

I have set forth the basic concepts on social cost, analyzed two common fallacies in the associated arguments for corrective public policies, and discussed the conditions required for the interpretation of economic behavior. The common fallacies are that

(i) the constraints assumed have largely been invalid, and
(ii) the observations reported have often been incorrect.

These, no doubt, have hindered the advancement of economics as a behavioral science. My criticism of the analyses in the Pigovian tradition should not be construed as an argument against government control. The thesis here is simply that any valuable application of economic theory must rest upon *careful empirical investigation to ensure that the facts are true, that the hypotheses are testable, and that the tests are performed.*

Analyses designed to assist policy making need not be inconsistent with those designed to interpret behavior. Any analysis which predicts the outcomes of a given policy will throw light on its desirability. Thus the fallacies regarded here as having marred the interpretation of behavior cannot be the result of analyses of policy. Perhaps the fallacies have derived from the economist's attempt to describe the world as it *ought* to be instead of the world as it *is*; perhaps the costs of careful research are prohibitively high; or perhaps economists are seeking recognition from government.

In the domain of a behavioral science, however, the pertinent question becomes not whether economists should participate in policy making, nor whether economic analysis could be useful in guiding policy decisions, nor whether economists have helped shape the world. The question is rather why public policies exist in the way they do, and why they vary in different economic systems. The answer to this question of the economic interpretation of political behavior requires an understanding of the real-world constraints relevant to government decision making. A recent shift of interest in that direction,[57] and a growing recognition of the importance of the analyses of government behavior in the theory of public choice, the economics of politics, presage a new momentum in the development of economics, particularly in industrial organization, public choice, and economic history. Although it lags by half a century behind Professor Pigou's pioneering works on social cost, the trend is encouraging.

[57][The main elements in the new direction in economics are indicated and analyzed in *The Economics of Politics* (London: IEA Readings 18, 1978.—ED.]

EPILOGUE

Externalities, Property Rights, and Public Policy: Private Property Rights or the Spoliation of Nature

JOHN BURTON

Senior Lecturer in Economics, Kingston Polytechnic

A central element of the "Cambridge tradition" of economics, handed down from Alfred Marshall[1] to A. C. Pigou[2] and J. M. Keynes,[3] is the idea that the study of economics is concerned (in Pigou's words) with "fruit as well as light": the formulation of rules for government policy as well as the scientific explanation of economic behavior. The main "fruit" of Pigou's labors as an economist was his highly influential analysis of divergences between private and social costs. In this country, Pigou ranks second only to his protégé John Maynard Keynes in his influence on opinion, at least among economists, on the appropriate agenda for government policy and intervention.

Was Pigou's "fruit" without blemish?

THE PIGOVIAN FORMULA

Pigou's contribution to the economic theory of government policy was based on armchair theorizing rather than empirical investigation. He diagnosed that the "private" costs (to the individual decision maker) of an activity could diverge from its "social" costs (to the decision maker and other members of society). The "external cost" or "external diseconomy" was the social cost minus the private cost. A divergence between

---

[1]Professor of Political Economy at the University of Cambridge, 1885–1908.

[2]Successor to Marshall's chair in 1908.

[3]Lecturer in Economics, University of Cambridge, 1908–20; elected Fellow of King's College, Cambridge in 1909; appointed Bursar of King's College in 1924.

private benefits and social benefits likewise gave rise to an "external benefit" or "external economy."

Each individual bases his decisions on the private costs and benefits that confront him—the costs and benefits to himself, not to society. The rational individual will thus not take into account the external "effects" (costs or benefits) of his actions. But the rule for *maximum* social efficiency in the allocation of resources, known as the Pareto rule,[4] is that each activity in society should be adjusted to the amount at which the marginal *social* benefit equals the marginal *social* cost. Thus Pigou concluded that, where private and social costs (or benefits) diverged, private decision making through market trading would lead to a misallocation of resources. The implication of Pigou's analysis was that government must intervene to correct such externalities, commonly referred to as "market failures." As a recent textbook puts it:

> as no attention is paid to these side-effects [i.e., externalities] in the market economy, the government must intervene with taxes and subsidies, regulation or other corrective measures in order to attain social efficiency.[5]

Note the "must"—this was the general thrust of the Pigovian analysis and deduction for policy.

Arthur Pigou and Tom Cobbleigh

Pigou's analysis of social cost has had enormous influence since its presentation in the early part of this century.[6] It has been, and is still being, handed down to generations of economics students in the textbooks. Professor Paul A. Samuelson's world-famous introductory text, *Economics,* instructed its readers as recently as 1973 that:

> *Whenever there are externalities, a strong case can be made for supplanting complete individualism by some kind of group action...The reader can think of countless...externalities where sound economics would*

---

[4] After Vilfredo Pareto, the Italian economist who originated this criterion for the optimal allocation of resources.

[5] P. Bohm, *Social Efficiency: A Concise Introduction to Welfare Economics* (London: Macmillan & Co., 1974), p. 32.

[6] A. C. Pigou, *Wealth and Welfare* (London: Macmillan & Co., 1912); *The Economics of Welfare* (London: MacMillan & Co., 1920).

> suggest some limitations on individual freedom in the in-
> terests of all.[7] (Italics in original.)

And also that:

> Since no one profit-maker has the incentive, or indeed the
> power, to solve problems involving "externalities," here
> is a clear case for some kind of public intervention.[8]

Numerous other examples of such statements can be cited.
Here are two more from recent textbooks for students:

> Where such external effects are important, a strong case
> can be made for public intervention, ranging all the way
> from regulation to subsidies and taxes, and, as in the case
> of public education, direct provision of the goods and
> services by the state.[9]

And

> *market prices. . . are simply unreliable indicators when
> there are externalities.* That. . . is the justification for
> government assuming the responsibility to have such ex-
> ternalities taken into account in production and consump-
> tion.[10] (Italics in original.)

Obeisance in public debate is also now almost always
made—though usually only vaguely—to the notions of social
costs and benefits whenever government intervention is ad-
vocated. In Britain the social costs/benefits argument has been
advanced as a justification for government action in:

- pollution controls and regulations
- town and country planning
- nationalization of industry
- "free" provision of health, welfare, and education services
- control of TV and radio broadcasting
- industrial subsidies and job "creation" measures
- protection of "infant" (supposedly prodigy) and "senile"
  (supposedly rejuvenatable) industries
- refuse collection by local authorities
- seat-belt legislation
- oil and mineral exploitation

[7]*Economics,* 9th ed. (New York: McGraw-Hill, 1973), p. 475.
[8]Ibid., p. 817.
[9]R. T. Gill, *Economics: A Text with Included Readings* (Pacific Palisades,
Calif.: Goodyear, 1973), p. 728.
[10]R. S. Eckaus, *Basic Economics* (Boston: Little, Brown, 1972), pp. 88–89.

- subsidies to the arts
- grants for R & D work
- agricultural protection
- keeping loss-making railway branch-lines and bus routes going
- "rescue" operations of large, failing companies (British Leyland, et al.)
- government purchase and free loan to users of prototype machine tools
- and Uncle Tom Cobbleigh and all...

The Pigovian social cost argument, carried to its logical conclusion, can be deployed as an argument for government intervention in anything and everything. For uncontracted or external effects are a pervasive phenomenon of social life. Walk down any street and you will be confronted with a vast number of external effects:

- the pleasing sight of a well-kept garden,
- the noise of children playing,
- exhaust fumes from passing cars,
- the smell of cooking,
- a pretty girl passing by,
- the roar of the traffic,
- canine deposits underfoot,
- the jostle of the crowd,
- advertisements on billboards (sometimes garish, sometimes informative and useful),
- and so on.

The simple Pigovian policy formula, carried to the logical extreme, implies that government should intervene, every second of our lives, to correct these myriads of externalities that surround us all the time.

This implication does not accord too well with common sense. If governments intervened to correct every externality, the entirety of the national effort would be eaten up many times over by resource-consuming intervention—and there would be no market activities left for "correction"! The old gray mare of the economy would collapse under the weight.

Common sense suggests there is something fundamentally wrong with the simple Pigovian policy formula.

THE FLAWS IN THE PIGOVIAN ANALYSIS

Enter R. H. Coase and the "Chivirla" School

Starting with a seminal analysis by Professor R. H. Coase of Chicago University published in 1960,[11] economic research has exposed the major flaws of the Pigovian analysis of social cost. This reexamination must be credited largely to the endeavors of the practitioners of two recently emerged, fast developing, and interconnected branches of economic analysis. The first is the property rights paradigm, erected by economists such as Professors Ronald Coase (at Chicago) and Steven Cheung (of the University of Washington), and Professors Armen Alchian and Harold Demsetz at the University of California at Los Angeles (UCLA). The other branch is public choice theory, led by economists such as Professors James Buchanan, Gordon Tullock, and Richard Wagner based at the Center for the Study of Public Choice at Virginia Polytechnic Institute and State University. Both of these new areas owe their development mainly to the work of U.S. economists. The IEA has contributed earlier to bringing these developments to the attention of a British readership.[12]

The property rights and public choice analyses have developed separately, but they are unified by a fundamental similarity of their basic hypotheses and methodology. Little violence is done to their respective positions—even if it is to the English language—if we talk of them, compositely, as the "Chivirla" school of economic analysis ("Chivirla" is the acronym arrived at by conflating the names of the universities at which these developments of economics have primarily taken place: Chicago, Virginia, UCLA).

Reflection on the central propositions in Professor Cheung's text will emphasize their implications for public policy and introduce further conclusions arising from research in the economics of property rights and public choice theory.

[11] R. H. Coase, "The Problem of Social Cost," *Journal of Law and Economics,* October 1960, pp. 1–44.

[12] For example, Armen A. Alchian, *Pricing and Society,* Occasional Paper 17, 1967; Gordon Tullock, *The Vote Motive,* Hobart Paperback 9, 1976; J. M. Buchanan, *The Inconsistencies of the National Health Service,* Occasional Paper 7, 1965; William A. Niskanen, *Bureaucracy: Servant or Master?,* Ho-

1. *The fundamentals: attenuation of property rights and transaction costs in the generation of external effects*

In his 1960 paper, Professor Coase showed in a remarkable tour de force of legal-economic analysis that, contrary to the Pigovian position, an external effect did *not* give rise to a misallocation of resources, provided there were no barriers to trade between its producer and consumer. If there are no transaction costs, and property rights are well defined and enforceable, the producer and consumer of the externality would have the familiar market incentive to negotiate a mutually beneficial trade between themselves and thus "internalize" (in effect, remove) the externality. The gains from such a trade would be maximized at the point where the marginal social cost was equal to the marginal social benefit. There would therefore be no misallocation of resources.

Consider a factory adjacent to a stream. The operation of the factory gives rise to a waste liquid, but to dispose of it via the stream the factory owner must obtain the permission of the stream owner, whose fishing would be adversely affected by the pollution of the factory. He could do this by compensating him. The solution would thus be found in the market. The factory owner would find it profitable to pay ("bribe") the stream owner up to the volume of waste emission where the marginal benefit to the factory owner (of disposed waste) was equal to the marginal cost (in reduced fish stock) to the owner of the stream.

A further, and revelatory, implication of Coase's analysis —known as the *neutrality theorem*—was that, under the assumed conditions of no barriers to trade, the outcome of the trading process would be the same, whether it was the producer or consumer of the externality who held the property right veto over the use of resources.[13] Suppose it were the factory owner who had the legal right to use the stream for disposal of waste, while the other party retained only the fishing rights in the stream. It would be the fisherman who would be willing to pay ("bribe") the factory owner to reduce the amount of waste

bart Paperback 5, 1973; Ralph Harris and Arthur Seldon, *Not From Benevolence . . .*, Hobart Paperback 10, 1977.
[13]Assuming that changes in the distribution of wealth do not alter the pattern of demand.

pumped into the stream, up to the point where the marginal benefit of better fishing equaled the marginal cost of disposing of the waste in another way. The result is the same as before: The market provides (or could provide if it were allowed) the solution by yielding the price at which the pollution is at least offset by the addition to output of goods and services.

The Coase analysis knocked the supports from under the Pigovian analysis, and pointed to entirely different implications for public policy. First, where there were no barriers to trade between the producer and consumer of an externality, government intervention is not called for because a "bargaining solution" would emerge: The externality would be "internalized" by trade between the affected parties, as shown by Professor Cheung in his study of the trade in pollination services of bees (above, section 6).

Second, it implied that the real trouble with social cost is not externalities (uncontracted effects) per se, but rather *barriers to trade* in the form of high transaction costs and attenuations of property rights that *prevent* a "bargaining solution" from emerging. The policy implications of this conclusion are discussed later.

2. *Externalities are reciprocal*

Pigou's analysis concentrated on the producer of the external effect. Likewise, his proposed solution was to be applied unilaterally to the producer. With an external diseconomy, the producer should be subjected to a tax equal to the size of the divergence between marginal social and marginal private costs. With an external economy, the producer should be given a subsidy equal to the difference between marginal social and marginal private benefit. The intention, in both, was that the full social costs or benefits should impinge on the *producer* of the externality.

Coase showed that an externality embodies a reciprocal relationship between *two* parties, the producer and the consumer, and that the consumer cannot be ignored in the analysis of, or policy on, externalities. Professors J. M. Buchanan and W. C. Stubblebine,[14] and Dr. Ralph Turvey,[15] developed further the

---

[14]"Externality," *Economica*, November 1962, pp. 371-84.
[15]"On Divergencies between Social Cost and Private Cost," *Economica*,

implications of Coase's analysis. They showed that the Pigovian solution for an externality—a tax or subsidy imposed *unilaterally* on its producer—did *not* result in an optimal allocation of resources, because the behavior of the consumer of the externality has to be altered as well. If an optimal allocation of resources is to result from an external diseconomy, not only must the producer of the externality take into account the costs imposed on the consumer, but the "consumer" must also take into account the costs imposed on the producer (i.e., benefits forgone) by any reduction of his activities resulting from the tax. And the "consumer" will not do this unless a "tax" is imposed on him for securing the benefits of the reduction in the externality.

The use of taxes and subsidies by government to correct for externalities requires not unilateral tax/subsidization on the producer(s) of external effects but *bilateral* taxation/subsidization of both the parties to the effect. In other words, the use of taxes and subsidies to correct for externalities could be administratively very complex—and *costly*. This conclusion is discussed further in 4 (below).

(Recently Professors S. A. Y. Lin and D. K. Whitcomb have sought to defuse this criticism.[16] They show, in a mathematically advanced treatment, that it would be possible in principle for government to operate a unilateral tax or subsidy scheme to correct for externalities. Their model assumes, however, that both firms and government have perfect and costless information, and also that the costs of policing are zero. The absurdity of the model is that, if these conditions were true, *there would be no need for government intervention to correct for externalities.* A "bargaining solution" would automatically emerge for every externality: They would all be internalized by trade.)

3. *Jointly supplied external benefits and costs*

Many external effects have both cost and benefit elements to them—as in Professor Cheung's examples of airports and neighborhood schools (above, section 3). A Pigovian tax/sub-

August 1963, pp. 309–13.
[16]"Externality Taxes and Subsidies," in S. A. Y. Lin, ed., *Theory and Measurement of Externalities* (New York: Academic Press, 1976), pp. 45–60.

sidy solution for such externalities would be even more ad-
minstratively complex—and *costly.*

4. *The administrative costs of government correction of
   "market failure"*

An implicit—but clearly untrue—assumption of the Pigovian analysis is that the cost of administering government intervention is zero (Cheung, section 6). Especially important is
the information cost of government intervention. Economists
do not always tell students and the public—or remind themselves—that the price system in the market is a relatively cheap
means of producing and transmitting information. It uses,

   first, the highly specialized and personal knowledge pos-
   sessed by individuals about their own preferences and circumstances;[17]
   second, a simple means of testing for the reliability of information about consumer preferences—the test of voluntary
   acceptance in the marketplace;[18] and,
   third, a simple means of business decision making—the
   yardstick of profit and loss.

Corrective government (nonmarket) actions cannot use these
low-cost means of acquiring information. Furthermore, to calculate the "ideal" (inefficiency-erasing) size of tax/subsidy necessary to offset an external cost/benefit precisely, the government would require perfect information of the *marginal* social
benefits and costs to all parties. The informational requirements—and their costs—are far larger than those of the price
system.

Moreover—and this is the decisive consideration—the costs
of administering "ideal" government correction of externalities would often dwarf the potential gains to society.

5. *Externalities arising from government "correction"
   of externalities*

It is often difficult, as Coase argued, to devise government
corrections of externalities that do not themselves create other

---

[17]F. A. Hayek, "The Use of Knowledge in Society," *American Economic
Review,* September 1945, pp. 519–30, reprinted in Hayek, *Individualism and
Economic Order* (Chicago: University of Chicago Press, 1948).

[18]H. Demsetz, "Contracting Cost and Public Policy," in Joint Economic

externalities. The Concorde supersonic airliner was heavily subsidized from tax funds on the ground, amongst others, that aircraft production is an advanced-technology industry that generates diffuse external benefits for other parts of the economy in "technological spinoff." This argument is highly doubtful in any event in terms both of its logical foundations and quantitative importance.[19] But there has been massive public controversy both in Great Britain and the United States about the (alleged) external costs of the Concorde in noise and atmospheric pollution.

6. *The motives of government: economic eunuchs?*

Another implicit assumption of the Pigovian analysis is that the political actors in government who devise market-correcting measures are "economic eunuchs" who act solely to maximize social efficiency without regard to their own utility, power, prestige, income, or vote appeal. This is another highly unrealistic assumption. Although the Roskill Commission's cost-benefit study[20] had suggested that Cublington was the least-cost site for the Third London Airport, the lobbying pressure from groups in the area led the government to drop this recommendation in favor of the Foulness site, where the antiairport lobbying had been weaker and less well organized.

A more useful hypothesis in the explanation of government behavior in real life than the Pigovian "eunuch" assumption is that the anticipated effect on voter behavior is an important (if not dominant) element in the choice calculus of governments. If government behavior is determined by vote considerations, the political mechanism will lead to the selection of "ideal" market-correcting government interventions *only* in the case where all political decisions require the *unanimous* consent of the electorate. If the choice by government (or decisions in a referendum on a single issue) is conducted under a simple majority voting system, the process of political choice may lead to

Committee, *The Analysis and Evaluation of Public Expenditures,* Washington, D.C.

[19]K. Hartley, *A Market for Aircraft* (London: IEA, Hobart Paper 57, 1974); and J. Jewkes, *Government and High Technology* (London: IEA, Occasional Paper 37, 1972).

[20]Commission on the Third London Airport, *Papers and Proceedings,* vol. 7, 1970, and the Commission's *Report,* HMSO, London, 1971.

the selection of government policies that fail to maximize social welfare.[21]

7. *The motives of intervention agencies*

The weakness of the Pigovian "eunuch" assumption about political behavior is reinforced by the fact that the bureaucrats who manage intervention agencies to "correct" market externalities have their own goals, independent of and separate from those of their political masters and the electorate. If, as Professor W. A. Niskanen has argued,[22] power, prestige, and income tend to be related to the size of the agency, bureaucrats have an incentive to expand the size of their budget allocation/agency. This will lead to "*over*correction" of externalities and an inefficient allocation of resources.

The Pigovian policy formula is thus dangerously oversimplistic as a rule for government policy on externalities. Furthermore, the "Chivirla" analysis points toward some different conclusions for policy making. They are discussed here in the context of the "problem of the commons": the tendency to overutilization of resources when there is unrestricted access to them.

THE "PROBLEM OF THE COMMONS": A PRIVATE PROPERTY SOLUTION?

Why are all externalities not "internalized" by trade? The answer, provided by the "Chivirla" analysis—and obscured by Pigou's—is that high transaction costs may emasculate property rights and prevent the emergence of a "bargaining solution." Externalities, in short, arise not from "market failures," but rather from the obstruction to market trading of high transaction costs.

In general, transaction costs take four main forms:
- the cost of acquiring information,
- the cost of negotiating the price to be paid,
- the cost of charging for the use of resources, and
- the cost (or impossibility) of excluding "free riders" from consuming resources they have not provided or paid for.

---

[21] These points are further developed by J. M. Buchanan in "The Coase Theorem and the Theory of the State," *Natural Resources Journal*, 1973, pp. 579-94.

[22] *Bureaucracy—Servant or Master?* (London: IEA, Hobart Paperback 5, 1973).

"The bulk of externality examples," Professor R. O. Zerbe has argued, "arise from situations in which exclusion costs are high,"[23] rather than from the other types of transaction costs. This is especially true in externalities affecting the natural environment.

Difficulties in excluding people who will not pay arise, in turn, from either the *lack* (or *attenuation*) of private property rights or from the *costs of enforcing* a private property right.

Environmental and conservation problems have to be seen in this light. All the most serious issues that environmentalists warn us about—atmospheric and oceanic pollution, the conservation of whales and other species threatened by extinction, the encroachment of the desert in the world's semiarid regions, and others—involve resources (the air, the sea, the land, or their inhabitants) in which private property rights are either considerably attenuated, ill-defined, or nonexistent.[24] Indeed, the air and the sea are classic examples of the polar *opposite* of private property—they are "common-property" (or "common-access") resources, to which everyone has equal access, so that they are rationed and used by the arbitrary device of "first come, first served (used)."

The serious problems of the environment and conservation exist where there is *common,* and not private, ownership. In Africa, for example, lions have been treated in the past as common property—"fair game" for anyone—with the result that their numbers have fallen drastically during the twentieth century. But in Great Britain lions are reared and held under private ownership (in game parks and zoos), and the British lion population has boomed. Indeed, British game parks are now exporting their surplus lions—to Africa! This is "taking coals to Newcastle" with a new twist.

An implication for conservation policy is that an alternative to government intervention could be investigated: enabling the market to work by removing attenuations of private property rights, where possible. Government may thus have a role to play in conservation by facilitating a "private property solu-

---

[23]"The Problem of Social Cost: Fifteen Years Later," in S. A. Y. Lin, *Theory and Measurement of Externalities,* p. 32.

[24]This argument is further developed in A. Alchian and H. Demsetz, "The Property Rights Paradigm," *Journal of Economic History,* 1973, pp. 16-65.

tion" rather than an "intervention solution." The former, indeed, has a number of *prima facie* advantages over the latter. It *uses* the relative efficiency of market trading—the price system—as a means of producing, testing, and utilizing information (my 4 above), while avoiding political and bureaucratic bias in resource allocation (6 and 7).

What is the scope for a "private property solution" to problems of conservation and the environment? It is illustrated here by a highly topical example: the spread of the desert in Africa.

The private property solution: the Sahelian tragedy

A colossal human tragedy has unraveled over recent years in the Sahelian (sub-Saharan) belt of Africa. This is a vast swath of arid and semiarid land running from one side of the continent to the other, from Senegal and Mauritania in West Africa, through Mali, Ghana, Nigeria, Upper Volta, Niger, Chad, Sudan, to Ethiopia and Somalia on the Horn, including parts of Kenya.

The trouble is the encroachment of the desert: the replacement of fertile by arid land. It is commonly estimated that some ten million people are currently facing starvation as a result. Mr. Kurt Waldheim, Secretary-General of the United Nations, has put it in stark terms: "The encroachment of the desert threatens to wipe four or five African countries from the map."

The immediate cause of this mass starvation is drought. Rainfall in the region has fallen below the annual average for some years. But this is only a temporary cause. The long-term tragedy of the Sahel is that its starvation and poverty are the consequences of Acts of *Man,* rather than short-term vagaries of climate ("Acts of God"). The underlying cause of the Sahelian tragedy is the misallocation of resources produced by attenuations of private property rights, exacerbated by well-meaning but disastrous *governmental* measures and United Nations advice on the promotion of agricultural productivity.

For millenia, under ancient and hallowed systems of property rights, the peoples of this belt have utilized a system of tribal or *communal* ownership of land. The inhabitants of the Sahel are primarily nomads and seminomads organized in tribes. Their economic system is pastoral: They tend moving flocks of camels, sheep, goats, and cattle. Each tribe has a recognized and carefully defined area of grazing and other rights, won by centuries of intertribal conflict, hallowed by custom, and now codified by the statutes of the African states that abut the Sahel. Over this territory encampments of the tribe move in a fixed (but sometimes complex) annual cycle from winter camp to summer pasture.

The replacement of fertile by barren land ("desertification") in sub-Saharan Africa is a classic, if tragic, example of the inefficiency in the use of resources resulting from the attenuation of private property rights. All trees, shrubs, and pasture are *common*-access resources, so no *individual* tribesman has an incentive to conserve them, or add to their stock. No individual can reap the returns of planting trees or sowing grass, which hold the soil together and prevent "desertification." The expected private benefits of planting activity are less than the social benefits under the system of communal tribal property rights. Conversely, as the land is communally owned, and allocated or utilized under a common-access or "first-come-first-served" system, the social costs of grazing or uprooting vegetation are higher than the private costs. Every tribesman has the incentive to get to good pasture first, and to graze it to the point of denudation, *without consideration of the external (social) costs.* Communal tribal ownership has thus produced divergences between private and social costs and benefits. The result has been overgrazing, denudation of the tree and shrub cover, soil erosion, and eventual "desertification."

This process has been gradual over thousands of years. In the past few decades it has been exacerbated by government attempts to increase pastoral productivity. The governments of sub-Saharan Africa, acting often under the guidance, and with the "expert" technical assistance, of the FAO (Food and Agricultural Organization) of the United Nations, have drilled boreholes to tap subterranean aquifers (water-bearing strata) and vaccinated animals to eliminate diseases prevalent amongst nomadic grazing flocks. These measures have not only completely failed to deal with the basic cause of "desertification" —the attenuation of private property rights—but have exacerbated it. Both the drilling and the vaccination have increased the size of grazing flocks and thus denuded the vegetative cover of the Sahel even further, and so encouraged encroachment of the desert. The concentrated press and trampling of animals around the new deep wells have, moreover, caused very severe erosion.

Solutions proffered for the now dire difficulties of sub-Saharan Africa (and other semiarid regions) at the recent UN Conference on Desertification, held at Nairobi in September 1977, were the usual monotonous fare served up at such meetings of the international bureaucracy. It was recommended that further "expert advice" on measures for the containment of the desert be made available to the governments of arid and semiarid regions under UN auspices (i.e., that the bureaucracy should be enlarged), that "training programs" for nomads be instituted to combat desertification (again, with UN help), and that there should be "multi-country integration" and "shared experience" of antidesertification schemes. None of these recommendations gets to the root of the trouble: the attenuation of private property rights in the use of land, vegetation, and water resources in the Sahel.

Government action to promote a *"private property solution"* is thus indispensable in stemming desertification in Sahelian Africa and other semiarid regions of the world. By the creation of a system of private property rights in land the inherently destructive tendencies of the existing system of communal tribal ownership would be countered and reversed. If individual tribesmen had property rights in land, i.e., *if they could legally exclude nonowners,* there would be an incentive to invest in planting grass, shrubs, and trees. The incentives would exist to roll back, rather than to create, desertification.

The lesson of Libya

That a "private property solution" holds the key to the containment of the desert is revealed by the lessons of Libyan agricultural history over the centuries.

Over 90 percent of the Republic of Libya is arid desert or semiarid steppe. But this was not always so.

> Historians claim that in Roman times Tripolitania [the western part of present-day Libya] was well-wooded and that grazing between the trees was productive.[25]

[25]A. Bottomley, "The Effect of Common Ownership of Land upon Resource Allocation in Tripolitania," *Land Economics,* 1963, fn. 17, p. 94.

Another study concludes that

> under the [Roman] empire the farmlands of Tripolitania reached a level of prosperity equalled neither before nor since.[26]

Cultivated farmland was far more extensive during the Roman era than before or after, and huge areas that have become desert were then green and plenteous. Tripolitania and Cyrenaica (the eastern Roman province) may not have been the granaries of the Roman empire, but the desert was then held far more extensively in check than under the following eras of Vandal, Berber, and Arab rule.

Historical research suggests that there was no wide variation in climatic conditions to account for the rolling back of the desert in the Roman era and the long-term trend to desertification thereafter. The answer seems to lie in the errors of human beings, not in the accidents of nature. Systems of common land ownership now account for the bulk of Libyan acreage, and have done so for over fifteen hundred years, since the Vandals expelled the Romans from Libya, circa AD 455. But under Roman rule the land was extensively farmed under a system of *private* property rights. During the early empire it was farmed primarily by Berber peasants and other small-holders such as retired soldiers who had been granted private property rights in plots of land. Later there also emerged *latifundia* (large privately-owned estates) worked by Berber serf labor. With land held privately, there was incentive to conserve vegetation, rather than to treat it as a "free good"). The benefits and costs of planting and grazing impinged upon the owner and not others: The externalities were "internalized."

Following the decline of Roman rule, the system of private property rights in land reverted to that of tribal ownership.

> The desert tribes...firmly [re-]established themselves over nearly all inland Tripolitania, which, by the end of the sixth century, had reverted to the old, pre-Roman nomadic pastoralism.[27]

The long-term consequences of that change in the system of property rights are written in the encroaching sands of the Libyan desert today.

[26] J. Wright, *Libya* (London: Ernest Benn, 1969), p. 54.
[27] Ibid., p. 73.

The philosopher George Santayana warns us that "those who cannot remember the past are condemned to repeat it."[28] Unless the lessons of Libyan history are remembered today, the nomads of sub-Saharan Africa will be condemned to their intensifying tragedy.

The limits to a private property solution

Can a redefinition of property rights provide a solution for all types of overexploitation of the environment arising from the "problem of the commons"?

The answer is "no." It is always possible in principle to define (i.e., set up) a system of private rights in property. But in some cases it would still be prohibitively expensive for the owners to police and enforce their rights, given the technical difficulties. Fish farming, for instance, is both technically feasible and commercially viable in some types such as oyster fishing (and probably also shore-based rearing of expensive fish such as turbot and sole). But the establishment of private rights of fishery in migratory fish seems so far technically infeasible.

On the other hand, the potential of the private property solution is larger than is commonly realized. The possibility is being discussed today of mining the manganese nodules[29] on the floors of the oceans which, it is estimated by geologists, constitute the largest mineral deposit on earth. If we continue to treat the ocean floors as *common* property resources (as now), the likelihood is that there would be overrapid exploitation of manganese nodules. But a *private* property solution seems quite feasible.[30] Allowing mining companies to establish private property rights in the nodules they discover would provide an incentive for them to reduce the rate of exploitation.

[28] *The Life of Reason,* vol. 1, chap. 12.

[29] These are geologically ancient ferro-manganese deposits formed by metallic-ion precipitation on the ocean floor.

[30] A discussion of the relative appropriateness of "private property" and "intervention" solutions to the exploitation of various types of presently common-access oceanic resources is provided in R. J. Sweeney, R. D. Tollison, and T. D. Willett, "Market Failure, the Common Pool Problem and Ocean Resource Exploitation," *Journal of Law and Economics,* April 1974, pp. 179–92.

CONCLUSIONS FOR PUBLIC POLICY

What conclusions may we draw for public policy?

First, the Pigovian policy rule—that externalities necessitate "corrective" government action—is dangerously oversimplistic. It is incorrect as a general rule for efficiency in resource allocation. Its application often leads to a *more* serious misallocation of resources than that arising from the externalities which government action is supposed to correct. The Pigovian analysis has provided a pretext for a long list of intervention measures in urgent need of reexamination.

Second, the Pigovian analysis contains an implicit bias toward "intervention solutions" for externalities, in the form of taxes, subsidies, regulations, and prohibitions.

Third, recognition of the fundamental role of *attenuations* of private property rights in generating externalities leads to consideration of the alternative policy of redefining property rights. The advantages of this approach are that it harnesses the incentives for individuals, and the relative cheapness of the price system as a means of generating and utilizing information, in the interests of conservation. "Intervention solutions," on the other hand, suffer from the defects of administrative complexity, high costs, and political and bureaucratic bias. A private property approach is not applicable in all instances, but insufficient attention has been paid in the past to the possibilities of applying it. It deserves further exploration by economists, technologists, and environmentalists.

The general conclusion for public policy is the classical one: Given the inherent defects, complexity, cost, and bias of an intervention solution, the general rule should be to let the price system deal with externalities wherever possible: by redefining property rights and removing barriers to trade due to externalities. Government intervention—domestic or supranational —is best kept as a "solution of the last resort": to be used only when and where high and irreducible transaction costs prevent the internalization of externalities by private action. Even on these grounds, government intervention must be carefully scrutinized, because the costs and external side-effects may outweigh the benefits. The mere existence of externalities thus does *not,* despite Professor Samuelson, provide "a clear case for some kind of public intervention."

RECOMMENDED READING

Alchian, Armen. *Economic Forces at Work*. Indianapolis: Liberty Press, 1977.

Browning, Edgar K. and Jacquelene M. *Public Finance and the Price System*. New York: Macmillan Co., 1979.

Buchanan, James M. *Cost and Choice*. Chicago: Markham, 1969.

———. "Property, Politics and Law: An Alternative Interpretation of Miller et al. v. Schoene." *Journal of Law and Economics* 15 (1972): 439.

———, ed. *Theory of Public Choice*. Ann Arbor, Mich.: University of Michigan Press, 1972.

———, and Thirlby, G. F., eds. *L.S.E. Essays on Cost*. London: Weidenfeld and Nicolson, 1973.

Cheung, Steven N. S. "Transaction Costs, Risk Aversion, and the Choice of Contractual Arrangements." *Journal of Law and Economics* 12 (April 1969): 23–42.

Coase, Ronald H. "The Problem of Social Cost." *Journal of Law and Economics* 3 (October 1960): 1–44.

Demsetz, Harold. "The Exchange and Enforcement of Property Rights." *Journal of Law and Economics* 7 (October 1964): 11–26.

———. "Some Aspects of Property Rights." *Journal of Law and Economics* 9 (October 1966): 61–70.

———. "Toward a Theory of Property Rights." *American Economic Review* 57 (May 1967): 347–59.

———. "When Does the Rule of Liability Matter?" *Journal of Legal Studies* 1 (January 1972): 13–28.

———. "Wealth Distribution and the Ownership of Rights." *Journal of Legal Studies* 1 (June 1972): 223–32.

Epstein, Richard A. *A Theory of Strict Liability.* Cato Paper No. 8. San Francisco: Cato Institute, 1980.

Furubotn, Eirik, and Svetozar, Pejovich. "Property Rights and Economic Theory: A Survey of Recent Literature." *Journal of Economic Literature* 10 (December 1972): 1137–62.

Gordon, H. Scott. "The Economic Theory of a Common-Property Resource: The Fishery." *Journal of Political Economy* 62 (February 1954): 124–42.

Hayek, Friedrich A. *Individualism and Economic Order.* Chicago: Gateway, 1972.

Kirzner, Israel M. *Competition and Entrepreneurship.* Chicago: University of Chicago Press, 1973.

Littlechild, Stephen C. "The Problem of Social Cost." In *New Directions in Austrian Economics,* edited by Louis M. Spadaro. Kansas City: Sheed Andrews and McMeel, 1978, pp. 77–93.

Posner, Richard A. *The Economic Analysis of Law.* Boston: Little, Brown and Co., 1972.

———. "A Theory of Negligence." *Journal of Legal Studies* 1 (June 1972): 29–96.

Regan, Donald. "The Theory of Social Cost Revisited." *Journal of Law and Economics* 15 (1972): 427.

Rizzo, Mario J., ed. *Time, Uncertainty, and Disequilibrium: Exploration of Austrian Themes.* Lexington, Mass.: Heath, 1979.

Rothbard, Murray N. "Justice and Property Rights." In *Property in a Humane Economy,* edited by Samuel L. Blumenfeld. La Salle, Ill.: Open Court, 1974.

ABOUT THE AUTHOR

Steven N. S. Cheung was born in Hong Kong in 1935 and received his doctorate in economics at the University of California at Los Angeles in 1967. He taught at the California State College at Long Beach from 1965 to 1967, where he received the Distinguished Teaching Award of the Board of Trustees of the California State Colleges. His dissertation on *The Theory of Share Tenancy* won him the Fellowship of Political Economy awarded by the University of Chicago in 1967, where he was appointed assistant professor of economics in the following year. In 1969 he went to teach at the University of Washington, since 1972 as a professor of economics.

Professor Cheung's main approach to research is empirical —he formulates hypotheses and then tests their implications against evidence. His conviction of the importance of property rights in affecting economic behavior has led to an almost exclusive focus on various aspects of transaction costs. As a price theorist, Professor Cheung typically specifies alternative sets of transaction costs in deriving his hypotheses, and then proceeds to test the implications through thorough investigations of the real-world situations.

His research comprises the economic explanation of pricing and contractual arrangements, including sharecropping, beekeeping rentals, ticket pricing, rent and price controls, patent and trade-secret licensing, and the pricing and contractual structures in various industries.

The Cato Papers

Reprinted by the Cato Institute, the Papers in this series have been selected for their singular contributions to such fields as economics, history, philosophy, and public policy.

Copies of the *Cato Papers* may be ordered from the Publications Department, Cato Institute, 747 Front Street, San Francisco, California 94111.